To Joe Giuliani,
Thanks for
your support,
George Leonard
March 30, 1982

DUCATION AND ECSTASY

EDUCATION

BY GEORGE B. LEONARD

AND ECSTASY

A DELTA BOOK

Published by
DELL PUBLISHING CO., INC.
1 Dag Hammarskjold Plaza
New York, N.Y. 10017

DELTA ® TM 755118, DELL PUBLISHING CO., INC.

ISBN: 0-440-52247-1

REPRINTED BY ARRANGEMENT WITH DELACORTE PRESS,
NEW YORK

MANUFACTURED IN THE UNITED STATES OF AMERICA

Thirteenth printing—February 1979

TO THE NEW GENERATION
AND MY VESTED INTEREST IN IT—
ELLEN, MIMI, LILLIE, EMILY

TABLE OF CONTENTS

EDUCATION AND ECSTASY

TEACHERS ARE OVERWORKED and underpaid. True. It is an exacting and exhausting business, this damming up the flood of human potentialities. What energy it takes to make a torrent into a trickle, to train that trickle along narrow, well-marked channels! Teachers are often tired. In the teachers' lounge, they sigh their relief into stained cups of instant coffee and offer gratitude to whoever makes them laugh at the day's disasters. This laughter permits a mo-

1. WHAT IS EDUCATION?

mentary, sanity-saving acknowledgment, shared by all, that what passes for humdrum or routine or boring is, in truth, tragic. (An hour, of which some fifty minutes are given up to "classroom control." One child's question unanswered, a hundred unasked. A smart student ridiculed: "He'll learn better." He learns.) Sweet laughter, shooting up like artesian water, breaks through encrusted perceptions and leaves a tear in a teacher's eye. A little triumph.

How do teachers bear their tragic task? They learn to look away. They hasten to a way of talking that lets them forget their problems. What cannot be solved is named. Once named, it does not seem to need a solution so urgently—perhaps never. James "acts out." (He is mad as hell at his teacher.) Melissa is an "underachiever." (So be it.) Susan suffers from "dyslexia." (That means—Shh! Don't let the parents in on it—"can't read." In certain early elementary classrooms, the disease is strangely absent. In others, a dozen or more children suffer from dyslexia. They can't read.)

Some teachers become actors. They generally enter this calling in the later grades, where the lecture system (best way to get information from teacher's notebook to student's notebook without touching the student's mind) flowers fully. Retiring behind a psychic proscenium arch, the actor-teacher is forever safe from the perils of education. His performance flourishes. He plays for laughs and outraged looks. Phantom applause accompanies his trip home to his wife and he cannot wait to go on stage again. Assured of a full house and a long run, he knows the critics will be kind. Those who give him a bad review will get a failing grade.

Principals have another out: their buildings. Concrete, glass, steel and wood stand still; their problems do not anguish the soul. I have visited a hundred schools and it is always the same. The visitor is directed to the office. There is an exchange of pleasantries, after which the principal escorts the visitor on a little tour around the plant. No matter that the visitor may have come only to work with Mrs. Morrison, the second-grade teacher down the hall. First the tour.

The principal walks briskly. "This is the multipurpose room. Notice the flexible dividers." In and out and down a corridor bright with what he calls "decorator colors." Classroom doors are open and the electricity of pent-up life crisscrosses the hall like lines of magnetic force. I am drawn to an open door. The principal hesitates, then presses on. I follow.

A boy sits on the floor of the hall next to a classroom door, his back against the wall, his head between his knees. He is a cliché—sweaty, tousled black hair, loose shirttail, a tennis shoe untied. As we pass, one big luminous eye appears between his knuckles and aims an accusation at me. Why has he been expelled from the company of his peers? I am drawn to the left. "On the right here is our new teachers' lounge." I go right. "I want you to feel free to use this room anytime you want. There's always coffee here, or you can just chew the rag with members of our staff."

We go on, into a classroom at last. It is a fifth grade, presided over by a stout maiden with glasses and reddish hair. Upon our appearance, the electricity within the room changes in a flash; the voltage of tension drops, the amperage of interest rises. Every face turns to us. "Excuse us, Miss Brown. I want our visitor to see one of our new classrooms." At the second seat of the second row, a boy's eyes drop from us to a notebook propped up on his desk. As the principal talks, I drift around to see what the boy is reading. Ah, a copy of *Popular Mechanics* hidden behind the notebook. He glances resentfully at me, then goes on reading, his eyes stubborn and dreamy. An aura of rare intelligence encircles him. I look away. He will need to keep all his stubbornness and all his dreams.

"If you'll notice the placement of the skylight, here, on the side of the room away from the windows, you'll see that the illumination is perfectly balanced at every desk." The principal is happy and I rejoice with him about the delicious, perfectly balanced flow of outdoor light into a room filled with beautiful children. But something disturbs me, a vinegary tingle at the back of my neck. *There is a witch in this room.* I see her near the back of the fourth row—milk-white skin, black hair falling onto a faded blue blouse, a band of freckles across the bridge of a small, sharp nose. Dark eyes with dilated pupils are fixed on me now, bold and direct, telling me that she knows, without words, everything that needs to be known about me. I return her stare, feeling that this girl, with an education she is not likely to get, might foretell the future, read signs, converse with spirits. In Salem she eventually would suffer the ordeal of fire and water. In our society she will be adjusted.

"When it gets dark outside," the principal is saying, "an electric-eye device—here—automatically compensates by turning on the lights to the requisite illumination." The girl's eyes never leave mine. She is a sorceress, too, for already she has created a whole new world inhabited only by the two of us. It is not a sexual world. What she has in mind—she could never put it into words—bypasses the erotic entirely. But later, when those talents of hers which do not fit the scientific-rationalist frame are finally extinguished, she may turn to sex. And she may become promiscuous, always seeking the shadow of an ecstasy and knowledge that by then she will remember only as a distant vibration, an inexplicable urge toward communion.

"You see, a classroom such as this can never become dark. The illumination will always be even." The principal, I realize, is telling Miss Brown that we are leaving. The girl has no intention of releasing my eyes. The principal is moving toward the door. For a moment I grow dizzy, then break the connection and follow my host out of the door, quickly reassuming the disguise we all must wear to travel safely in the world that I and the principal and most of us customarily pretend is real.

I compliment the principal but I know the illumination in that room will never be even. A classroom, any classroom, is an awesome place of shadows and shifting colors, a place of unacknowledged desires and unnamed powers, a magic place. Its inhabitants are tamed. After years of unnecessary repetition, they will be able to perform their tricks—reading, writing, arithmetic and their more complex derivatives. But they are tamed only in the manner of a cage full of jungle cats. Let the right set of circumstances arise, the classroom will explode.

What a job this is we give our teachers! No wonder they insulate their perceptions, learn to speak strange tongues, become thespians. Some of them turn sadists—the temptation is great—but we shall not speak of them; conscious cruelty is rare in today's schools. The present classroom situation is more likely to create curious adaptations, in which it is hard to puzzle out who is doing what to whom.

Take the case of the strange sound that came from a classroom door during one of my introductory tours around an elementary school. From a distance, the sound might have been a red-hot poker plunging into ice water or a Southern pine snake striking a rabbit. It was repeated at irregular intervals of about five to ten seconds, sometimes rising climactically to an even more rapid pace. At first I thought something was seriously wrong with the heating system, but as we drew nearer, I could make out a teacher's shrill, strained voice playing counterpoint with the hissing and I realized she was using it to quiet her class. "Now—SHHH!—boys and girls, mammals—SHHH!—are the only members of the animal—SHHH!—kingdom that have coats of hair—SHHH!—or—SHHH!—fur—SHHH!" I lingered at the door for only a moment, but it was long enough to make me slightly ill. During the first days of my visit to that school—I was to spend a couple of weeks in another classroom—my imagination kept going back to the room of the hiss. I wondered how the children's nervous systems could stand up under such a barrage. I envisioned them going home to sit trembling in a corner, their guts all shriveled with shame.

I was mistaken. Several days later, after most teachers in the school had become accustomed to my presence, I entered the room. The teacher, a tall, handsome woman of Scandinavian descent, welcomed me with a little smile, then went right on with her cacophony. It took only a few minutes for me to realize that the children were by no means humiliated and nerve-wracked. They seemed slightly drugged but quite intent, like jazz musicians on marijuana. The teacher's SHHH! was not controlling them at all. Far from it. They were, with elegant, unconscious cooperation, eliciting the sound from her. She was their puppet; they pulled her strings by creating precisely enough disturbance, superbly timed, to keep her SHHH-ing at a maximum rate. The children's skill at this task honored the human potential; they probably slept well at night.

Still later, I met the teacher in the lounge. This charming woman displayed not the least sign of her classroom behavior. Nor did the principal give the matter more than a passing thought. When I discussed it with him near the end of my stay, he took a few moments to bring the sound to his consciousness. He then acknowledged it to himself and me, smiled slightly and commented, not without relevance, that she was "a fine woman, a teacher I can count on."

(To learn is to change. Education is a process that changes the learner.)

Do not blame teachers or their administrators if they fail to educate, to change their students. For the task of *preventing* the new generation from changing in any deep or significant way is precisely what most societies require of their educators. Perhaps it is enough that schools should go on with their essentially conservative function: passing on the established values and skills of the past. Perhaps schools should not change but civilize (restrict human behavior) while superimposing skills and polish. Who would experiment with children's lives?

But something is wrong. Every wind-tee we raise into the gales of the future tells us that people had better find new ways of acting, of relating, of dealing with their environments. Just to survive, it appears, we need a new human nature; so we find ways of talking about "the gap between technology and sociology." We sense that our salvation lies in education; so we trifle around the edges of things pedagogical and call it "revolution." When nothing much happens, we turn upon our educators with a harshness that dishonors not them, but ourselves. We damn them as mere baby-sitters when this is the function we most avidly press upon them. We ridicule them for preoccupation with "method" when no really workable methods have been provided them and, indeed, this is what they most desperately need. We slander them, slyly, as somehow wanting in the finely honed intellects of their detractors or, archly, as "lower-middle-class-upward-mobile," when the ability to score high on those culturally rigged ratings we call "intelligence tests" has little to do with the ability to educate and indeed sometimes signifies a doctrinaire, inhuman rigidity that resists change.

No, educators are not the culprits. They are the valiant slaves of our society, condemned to perpetuate the very system that victimizes them. They are sometimes bewildered, sometimes angry, often tired because—at a time of harrowing cultural upheaval, with practically an entire continental civilization's children in school—the mutual deception between them and their masters is wearing thin. If education is a process that causes real change, not just in one's ability to manipulate symbols, but in every aspect of one's being, then what today's educators are called upon to do may be many things, but it is not education.

And yet there are moments of learning, even in school. "Have you ever noticed," a teacher said, out of the blue, "how sometimes there are teachable days?" The teachers' lounge fell suddenly silent. "I know sometimes *they* are teachable," a second teacher mused. "Some days it's different," the first teacher continued. "The whole thing's different. I don't know why."

How many of those times do you remember? *Something happens.* A delicate warmth slides into parts of your being you didn't even realize were cold. The marrow of your bones begins to thaw. You feel a little lurch as your own consciousness, the teacher's voice, the entire web of sound and silence that holds the class together, the room itself, the very flow of time all shift to a different level. And suddenly it is Christmas morning, with students and teacher exchanging delightful gifts while bells silently chime; the old furniture around the room reflects a holiday gleam; your

classmates' eyes sparkle and snap like confetti and you realize with the certainty of music how rare and valuable each
inhabitant of that room has become, has always been. Or
you find yourself trembling slightly with the terror and
joy of knowledge, the immensity of existence and pattern
and change. And when it ends and you must go, you reel
from the room with flushed face, knowing you will never
again be quite the same. You have learned.

How many teachable days? One out of a hundred? Then
you are of the favored.

But there are teachers, a few of them, who can make
something happen almost every day. I have seen more than
my share of those masters who, in terms of our small expectations, seem to be miraculously gifted. No principal or
superintendent misses a chance to show me such a teacher
if one is anywhere around. I have sat in a child's miniature
chair in the back of a third-grade room, my heart racing,
while the class learned simple arithmetic. And I have been
changed.

How many such teachers in your lifetime? How many
who changed your life? Two? Three? Count yourself lucky.

So here we are. And there our children sit, counting out
a few seconds of learning for every hour of waiting for a
bell to ring, waiting for a kind of teacher they may have
never known, waiting for *something to happen*. If only
their waiting could be merely neutral, we wish. If only
they could sit there, learning *nothing*, without ill effects!
"Look upon every delay as an advantage," Rousseau wrote;
"it is gaining a great deal to advance without losing anything." He sought some way "to do nothing yourself, . . .
to prevent anything being done by others, . . . to bring up
your pupil healthy and robust to the age of twelve years
without his being able to distinguish his right hand from
his left."

But no one can be rescued from learning; learning is what human life is. Brain researcher John Lilly and others have tried to cut off the connections between the inner self and the world of the senses from which the stuff of learning comes. In these sensory-deprivation experiments, the subject is suspended, nude, in a tank of tepid water. His eyes are blindfolded, his ears are plugged; he breathes through a face mask. He becomes, as far as possible, a disembodied brain. But the brain is not content to rest. It reshuffles past learning, builds rich new inner worlds in which the self seems to move and learn. "When I went in the tank," Dr. Lilly told me, "I could will myself into the center of a giant computer. I could see the connections reaching out from me in every direction in vivid colors. Or, if I wished, I could ski across the top of the Andes, skimming from one peak to another."

There are no neutral moments. Even in those classrooms where the education some of us might hope for is impossible, a kind of shadowy, negative learning is going on. Some pupils learn how to daydream; others, how to take tests. Some learn the petty deceptions involved in cheating; others, the larger deceptions of playing the school game absolutely straight (the well-kept notebook, the right answer, the senior who majors in good grades). Most learn that the symbolic tricks their keepers attempt to teach them have little to do with their own deeper feelings or anything in the here and now. The activity that masquerades under the ancient and noble name of "education" actually seems to serve as a sort of ransom to the future, a down payment toward "getting ahead"—or at least toward not falling behind. Lifetime-earnings figures are pressed upon potential high-school dropouts. These figures seem to show that giving an acceptable interpretation of "Ode on a Grecian Urn" somehow means you will live in a better suburb and drive a bigger car. A vision of Florida retirement superimposes itself on every diagram in plane geometry. Some students refuse to pay the ransom, and you should not be surprised that these students may be what the society itself calls the "brighter" ones. (According to Dr. Louis Bright, director of research for the U. S. Office of Education, high-school dropouts in large cities where the figures are available have higher IQs than high-school graduates.) But dropouts and graduates alike have had plenty of practice in fragmenting their lives—segregating senses from emotions from intellect, building boxes for art and abstractions, divorcing the self from the reality and the joy of the present moment. No need for obscure psychological explanations for modern man's fragmentation; that is what his schools teach.

Perhaps this has been so ever since education was first formalized. Historian Arnold Toynbee traces the disintegration of the Chinese Empire under the Ts'in and Han Dynasties as well as that of the Roman Empire, in part, to their attempts to extend formal education from the privileged minority to a wider circle. "One reason," Toynbee wrote, "was that the former privileged minority's traditional system of education was impoverished in the process of being disseminated. It degenerated into a formal education in book learning divorced from a spontaneous apprenticeship for life. . . . In fact, the art of playing with words was substituted for the art of living."

In more primitive cultures, the Polynesian, for example, education was sacramental. Every aspect of life, every act of living was related, and life's procedures were learned in a manner simultaneously more intense and more casual than would seem possible in a formal institution. All things were observed and experienced in unity. The educational institutions of Western civilization, on the other hand, have almost always been formalistic and symbolic to the extreme. When the Renaissance academies took the Roman educator Quintilian for their model, they managed to adopt his most negative and stultifying precepts, leading to purely verbal training in ancient literature— even though Quintilian's was a specialized school for orators.

Until relatively recent times, however, only a tiny proportion of the West's population ever saw the inside of an academy. (As recently as 1900, less than ten percent of American sixteen-year-olds were in school.) Education for the vast majority, though less sacramental and ecstatic, resembled that of the Polynesians. Under the tutelage of such stable institutions as the family, the farm, the village, the church and the craft guild, the ordinary young Westerner served his apprenticeshp for living—limiting, perhaps, but all of a piece. As for the aristocrat, he lived and learned under the sure guidance of class tradition and accepted formal education primarily as an instrument for fortifying class lines. Better than badges and plumes were Latin and Greek, maintained, under the fiction of teaching "thinking," for centuries after the world's literature was available in translation. (All attempts to prove that the study of Latin improves thinking skills have failed.) A school accent served as well as a school tie in bolstering those barriers between people which seemed so necessary in building and maintaining a militaristic, colonial empire.

The successive historical events we know as the Enlightenment, the process of democratization, the Industrial Revolution and the explosive developments of consumerism and leisure weakened the prime educating institutions of the past (family, farm, village, church, guild), leaving successively more of the younger generation's total education-for-living to the schools and colleges. The young crowded into classrooms and were led away from life.

Reformers tried to stop the fragmentation. The greatest among them was John Dewey. We have at last reached a hillock in time from which we can look across a lot of pointless controversy and view this man's genius with a certain clarity and dispassion. Dewey sought a unity in life. He recognized that education is a process of living and not a preparation for future living. He believed that education is the fundamental method of social progress and reform. He provided a philosophical underpinning for the Progressive Education movement which, simply stated, saved the American public-school system by making it just flexible and forgiving enough to accommodate the children of immigrants, poor farmers and other followers of the American dream.

But Dewey did not provide educators with the hardhoned tools of true reform. Seduced by the psychology of his time, he enjoined teachers to spend more energy helping children form "images" than making them learn certain things. More disabling yet, he was fascinated with the notion of "interests," which he felt would automatically manifest themselves in children when they were *ready* to learn something. This notion, somewhat misinterpreted, led a generation of teachers to wait for children to show signs of "interest" before they moved ahead and thereby woefully to underrate their capacity for learning. Teachers found further justification for just waiting in the work of developmental psychologists who followed Dewey. These good-hearted doubters are still around with stacks of studies to show us precisely what children *cannot* do until this age or that age. Their studies become worthless, as we shall see in the next chapter, when children are placed in learning environments designed to let them crash through all the ceilings erected by the past. Progressive education was a useful, humane and sometimes joyful reform, but it was not the true revolution in education that the times then needed and now demand. The worst of that movement may be summed up in one sentence: It is as cruel to bore a child as to beat him.

(Learning eventually involves interaction between learner and environment, and its effectiveness relates to the frequency, variety and intensity of the interaction.)

For the most part, the schools have not really changed. They have neither taken up the slack left by the retreat of the past's prime educators nor significantly altered the substance and style of their teaching. The most common mode of instruction today, as in the Renaissance, has a teacher sitting or standing before a number of students in a single room, presenting them with facts and techniques of a verbal-rational nature. Our expectation of what the human animal can learn, can do, can be remains remarkably low and timorous. Our definition of education's root purpose remains shortsightedly utilitarian. Our map of the territory of learning remains antiquated: vocational training, homemaking, driving and other "fringe" subjects, themselves limiting and fragmenting, have invaded the curriculum, but are generally considered outside the central domain of "education." This domain, this venerable bastion, is still a place where people are trained to split their world into separate symbolic systems, the better to cope with and manipulate it. Such "education," suprarationalistic and analytical to the extreme, has made possible colonialism, the production line, space voyaging and the H-bomb. But it has not made people happy or whole, nor does it now offer them ways to change, deep down, in an age that cries out with the urgency of a rocket's flight, "Change or die."

All that goes on in most schools and colleges today is only a thin slice, as we shall see, of what education can become. And yet, our present institutions show a maddening inefficiency even in dealing with this thin slice. In recent years, there has been a small net gain in American students' performance in the basic subjects. But this has been accomplished only at the cost of a large increase in gross effort—more and more homework assigned under threat of more and tougher exams to force students to learn, on their own, what most of today's teachers have long since realized they cannot teach them. A visitor from another planet might conclude that our schools are hell-bent on creating—in a society that offers leisure and demands creativity—a generation of joyless drudges.

There are signs the school will not succeed in this drab mission. Already, the seeds of a real change are germinating—on college campuses, in teachers' associations, in laboratories of science, in out-of-the-way places that will be discussed in later chapters. This reform would bypass entirely the patchwork remedial measures (Spanish in second grade, teachers in teams, subject matter updated) that presently pass for reform. It cuts straight to the heart of the educational enterprise, in and out of school, seeking new method, content, idiom, domain, purpose and, indeed, a new definition of education. Far from decrying and opposing an onrushing technology, it sees technology as an ally, a force that can as easily enhance as diminish the human spirit. Avoiding hard-and-fast assumptions of its own, it is rigorous in questioning some of the automatic assumptions of the past. It is a new journey. To join it, you had best leave your awe of history behind, open your mind to unfamiliar or even disreputable solutions if they are the ones that work, look upon all systems of abstractions as strictly tentative and throw out of the window every prior guideline about what human beings can accomplish.

The prospects are exhilarating, though it is becoming dangerous to write about them if only because nowadays it is so hard to stay ahead of reality. Let us assume the future will surprise us; and, so assuming, speculate only about what is already coming to pass. For example, the following prospects are in the realm of possibility:

● Ways can be worked out to help average students learn whatever is needed of present-day subject matter in a third or less of the present time, pleasurably rather than painfully, with almost certain success. Better yet, the whole superstructure of rational-symbolic knowledge can be rearranged so that these aspects of life's possibilities can be perceived and learned as unity and diversity within change rather than fragmentation within an illusory permanence.

● Ways can be worked out to provide a new apprenticeship for living, appropriate to a technological age of constant change. Many new types of learning having to do with crucial areas of human functioning that are now neglected or completely ignored can be made a part of the educational enterprise. Much of what will be learned tomorrow does not today have even a commonly accepted name.

● Ways can be worked out so that almost every day will be a "teachable day," so that almost every educator can share with his students the inspired moments of learning now enjoyed by only the most rare and remarkable.

● Education in a new and greatly broadened sense can become a lifelong pursuit for everyone. To go on learning, to go on sharing that learning with others may well be considered a purpose worthy of mankind's ever-expanding capacities.

(Education, at best, is ecstatic.)

If education in the coming age is to be, not just a part of life, but the main purpose of life, then education's purpose will, at last, be viewed as central. What, then, is the purpose, the goal of education? A large part of the answer may well be what men of this civilization have longest feared and most desired: *the achievement of moments of ecstasy*. Not fun, not simply pleasure as in the equation of Bentham and Mill, not the libido pleasure of Freud, but ecstasy, *ananda*, the ultimate delight.

Western civilization, for well-known historical reasons, has traditionally eschewed ecstasy as a threat to goal-oriented control of men, matter and energy—and has suffered massive human unhappiness. Other civilizations, notably that of India, have turned their best energies toward the attainment of ecstasy, while neglecting practical goals—and have suffered massive human unhappiness. Now modern science and technology seem to be preparing a situation where the successful control of practical matters and the attainment of ecstasy can safely coexist; where each reinforces the other; and, quite possibly, where neither can long exist *without* the other. Abundance and population control already are logically and technologically feasible. At the same time, cybernation, pervasive and instantaneous communication and other feedback devices of increasing speed, range and sensitivity extend and enhance man's sensory apparatus, multiplying the possibilities for understanding and ecstasy as well as for misunderstanding and destruction. The times demand that we choose delight.

Do discipline and mastery of technique stand in opposition to freedom, self-expression and the ecstatic moment? Most Western educators have acted as if they did. Strange, when there exist so many models of the marriage between the two. Take the artistic endeavor: the composer discovers that the soul of creation transcends the body of form only when form is his completely. The violinist arrives at the sublime only through utter mastery of technique. The instruments of living that are now coming into our hands —rich, responsive and diverse—require mastery. The process of mastery itself can be ecstatic, leading to delight that transcends mastery.

The new revolutionaries of education must soothe those who fear techniques no less than those who fear delight. Many a liberal educational reform has foundered on lack of specific tools for accomplishing its purposes—even if a tool may be something as simple as knowing *precisely when* to leave the learner entirely alone. Education must use its most powerful servant, technique, in teaching skills that go far beyond those which submit to academic achievement tests. Even today, as will be seen, specific, systematic ways are being worked out to help people learn to love, to feel deeply, to expand their inner selves, to create, to enter new realms of being.

What is education? The answer may be far simpler than we imagine. Matters of great moment and processes that affect our lives at the very heart are generally less obscure and mysterious than they at first appear. The travels of celestial bodies, once requiring the efforts of a pantheon of gods, now follow a few easy formulas. Chemical reactions explained by essences, vapors, phlogiston became easier to understand when reduced to a single variable: weight. Mankind's most awesome mystery, fire, once understood, could be handled by little children. Throughout history, the way to understanding, control and ecstasy has been a long, sinuous journey toward simplicity and unity.

To learn is to change. Education is a process that changes the learner.

The first part of a simple, operational definition of education calls on the educator to view his work as consequential, not theoretical or formalistic. Looking for *change* in his student (and himself) as a measure, he will discover what is important in his work and what is waste motion. Asking himself, "What has changed in the student, and me, because of this particular experience?," he may have to answer that what has changed is only the student's ability to recite a few more "facts" than he could before the session. He may find that the student has changed in wider and deeper ways. He may have to admit that the student has hardly changed at all or, if so, in a way that no one had intended. In any case, he will not ask himself the *wrong* questions ("Wasn't my presentation brilliant?" "Why are they so dumb?").

Looking for the *direction and further consequences* of the change, he will be forced to ask whether it is for the good of the student, himself and society. In doing this, the educator will discover he has to become sensitive to what is happening to the student at every moment, and thereby will become a feeling participant in the circle of learning. Viewing learning as anything that changes the learner's behavior, the educator will expand his domain a thousand-fold, for he will realize that there are hardly any aspects of human life that cannot be changed, educated. He will see clearly that, if the educational enterprise limits itself to what is now ordinarily taught in classrooms, it will be pursuing failure in the coming age.

Learning involves interaction between the learner and his environment, and its effectiveness relates to the frequency, variety and intensity of the interaction.

Guided by this second part of the definition, the educator will pay far closer attention to the learning environment than ever before in education's history. The environment may be a book, a game, a programmed device, a choir, a brainwave feedback mechanism, a silent room, an interactive group of students, even a teacher—

but in every case, the educator will turn his attention from mere *presentation* of the environment (a classroom lecture, for example) to the *response* of the learner. He will study and experiment with the learning process, the series of responses, at every step along the way, better to utilize the increasing capacities of environment and learner as each changes. Observing the work of what have been called "master teachers" in this light, he will find that their mysterious, unfathomable "artistry" actually comprises a heightened sensitivity to student responses plus the use of personally developed, specific, flexible techniques. The educator will work out ways to help every teacher become an "artist."

Education, at best, is ecstatic.

The first two parts of the definition need the third, which may be seen as a way of praising learning for its own sake. And yet, it goes further, for the educator of the coming age will not be vague or theoretical about this matter. As he loses his fear of delight, he will become explicit and specific in his pursuit of the ecstatic moment. At its best, its most effective, its most unfettered, the moment of learning is a moment of delight. This essential and obvious truth is demonstrated for us every day by the baby and the preschool child, by the class of the "artist" teacher, by learners of all ages interacting with new learning programs that are designed for success. When joy is absent, the effectiveness of the learning process falls and falls until the human being is operating hesitantly, grudgingly, fearfully at only a tiny fraction of his potential.

The notion that ecstasy is mainly an inward-directed experience testifies to our distrust of our own society, of the outer environment we have created for ourselves. Actually, the varieties of ecstasy are limitless, as will be seen in the coming chapters. The new educator will seek out the possibility of delight in every form of learning. He will realize that solving an elegant mathematical problem and making love are different classes in the same order of things, sharing common ecstasy. He will find that even education now considered nothing more than present drudgery for future payoff—learning the multiplication tables, for example—can become joyful when a skillfully designed learning environment (a programmed game, perhaps) makes the learning quick and easy. Indeed, the skillful pursuit of ecstasy will make the pursuit of excellence, not for the few, but for the many, what it never has been —successful. And yet, make no mistake about it, excellence, as we speak of it today, will be only a by-product of a greater unity, a deeper delight.

This is a book about education, but that doesn't mean it is just about schools. The next four chapters, in fact, touch upon schools as we know them only in passing. Chapter II, "The Human Potential," explores the capabilities of the human organism. Chapter III, "The Naked Environment," shows how the outer environment, sometimes unperceived, can limit and also can enhance the development of greater human capability. Chapter IV, "The Chain of Learning," treats the interaction between the environment and the organism, be it man or animal, and, most particularly, attempts to assay the educational effects of the Civilized Epoch. Chapter V, "The Rogue as Teacher," shows how certain individuals have managed to get around the civilized strictures and suggests what we may learn from them. After that, it is back to school again, but not in a way you might at first imagine.

Here, then, is a vision of hope in an age when hope does not come easy, a treatise not only on things as they are, but as they can be and are becoming.

WHO IS THIS CREATURE we would educate so joyfully? What are his capacities? Can he really be changed? Will great efforts yield us great gains? History tells us more than we want to know about what is wrong with man, and we can hardly turn a page in the daily press without learning the specific time, place and name of evil.

But perhaps the most pervasive evil of all rarely appears in the news. This evil, the waste of human potential, is

2. THE HUMAN POTENTIAL

particularly painful to recognize, for it strikes our parents and children, our friends and brothers, ourselves. "I believe," wrote James Agee, "that every human being is potentially capable, within his 'limits,' of fully 'realizing' his potentialities; that this, his being cheated and choked of it, is infinitely the ghastliest, commonest, and most inclusive of all the crimes of which the human world can accuse itself. . . . I know only that murder is being done against nearly every individual on the planet."

To doubt is less painful than to rage. Throughout much of history, the safe, the authoritative, the official viewpoint has pronounced man limited, flawed and essentially unchangeable. Each age has found ways of comforting men with pessimism. Christ believed in the human potential, but the Grand Inquisitor told Him his Church could not. Sigmund Freud composed a sinuous allegory on the theme of Original Sin, so rich in literary possibilities that three generations of artists and healers could revel in its darkness. Tragedy has seemed more profound than comedy; "human nature" becomes "the Human Condition." The wisdom of Ecclesiastes is the wisdom of limitations. Accept limits, the wise men say, to keep from overreaching yourselves or going mad with hope.

But hope and the awareness of wasted potential have never really faded from consciousness. Ever since the race of man first learned to wonder, men have been haunted by this irrepressible dream: that the limits of human ability lie beyond the boundaries of the imagination; that every human being uses only a tiny fraction of his abilities; that there must be some way for everyone to achieve far more of what is truly his to achieve. History's greatest prophets, mystics and saints have dreamed even more boldly, saying that all men are somehow one with God. The dream has survived history's failures, ironies and uneven triumphs, sustained more by intuition than by what our scientific-rationalist society calls "facts."

Now, however, the facts are beginning to come in. Science has at last turned its attention to the central questions of human capability, has begun the search for a technology as well as a science of the human potential. Men in varied fields, sometimes unknown to each other, sometimes disagreeing on method, philosophy and even language, are coming to startlingly similar conclusions that make pessimism about the human prospect far more difficult than before. These men—neurologists, psychologists, educators, philosophers and others—are making what may well be the century's biggest news. Almost all of them agree that people now are using less than ten percent of their potential abilities; some put the figure at less than one percent. The fact of the matter is that *anyone* who makes a responsible and systematic study of the human animal eventually feels the awe that moved Shakespeare to write: "What a piece of work is a man! how noble in reason! how infinite in faculty!"

Start with the brain. This marvelous piece of matter, now so intent upon analyzing itself, is the most complex organized entity in the known universe. Plato called the mind "a gift of Memory, the mother of the Muses," and guessed it to be a block of wax on which the perceptions were printed, preserved and modified. Since Plato's time, man's concept of how his brain works has evolved considerably and is currently undergoing revolutionary revisions.

The brain may be viewed as a sort of computer. Each of its ten billion neurons (brain cells), if sufficiently excited, may fire a burst of electricity. This burst may help excite a nearby neuron so it, too, will fire, and so on, until a long chain of firing neurons carries a message that may command a muscle to move, may produce the sensation of "green," may help form a "memory trace" or may be an element in the discovery of an abstract mathematical formula.

In this commonly held view of the brain, each neuron has only two possibilities, to fire or not to fire. Even so, there are enough possible combinations of the billions of neurons to account for the behavior exhibited by Beethoven in composing the late quartets, by Milton in writing *Paradise Lost* and by Einstein in formulating the General Theory of Relativity—with plenty of unused ability left over.

But that, as it turns out, is only the beginning. To peer into the more complex workings of the brain requires a computer that fills a room and a tiny electric probe that pierces a single neuron. Several research teams are using these and other modern tools to deduce new concepts of information processing and storage in the central nervous system. The new models of the brain that emerge from this work are to the old computer-like brain as poetry is to grammar. Dr. W. Ross Adey and his colleagues at the Space Biology Laboratory of UCLA's Brain Research Institute have discovered hitherto unsuspected electrical happenings deep within the brain. They have found complex wave patterns during learning and recall. They have measured the changing resistance to electricity across certain key brain areas and again have found significant patterns during the learning process. This electricity, these waves flow not through the neurons themselves but through the softer neuroglial cells that surround them and the jellylike substance that fills the space between the cells. Such activity may well constitute an exceedingly subtle means for influencing the *probability* of neurons' firing across a relatively wide area of the brain.

"The on-off of neurons," Dr. Adey told me, "is the minimum way the brain has of operating." Adey's associates have gone as far as to prepare a sort of weather map of the mind, taking several ongoing brain waves from an astronaut candidate and, with a computer's help, charting them all together on a piece of paper. Looking at one of these charts, we may visualize changes in "mood." Just where the would-be astronaut's task becomes unexpectedly more difficult, we see what might be termed a sharp "cold front" followed by "thunderstorms."

"The brain," Dr. Adey said, "is not a telephone switchboard that operates only when signals arrive from outside. The switchboard is always flooded. It is altered in the whole. And it is altered by subtle, qualitative changes in the incoming signals, not by the presence or absence of lights on the switchboard, but by shifts of brightness or color."

Adey's hypothesis dovetails with recent news from the laboratories of the biochemists. Every living cell, including brain cells, contains DNA (deoxyribonucleic acid), the complex genetic molecules that pass along the blueprints of the species. Somewhat similar molecules of another substance, RNA (ribonucleic acid), serve as messengers for the DNA, informing the proteins in the body what and how to build. The RNA in the brain's cells, it now seems, has another talent, one that helps explain the brain's remarkable capacities. Each RNA molecule is a storehouse of information, a microscopic library. What if the RNA molecules *inside* the brain cells could be altered by events taking place *outside* the cells? What if the temporary electrical and chemical happenings going on throughout the brain could, by changing RNA, make a lasting change inside the brain cells? If so, it would be much easier to explain one of life's great mysteries: how the behavior of a living thing can be changed for more than a moment by its environment—in other words, how it learns.

Such an explanation is gathering shape in the work of

such chemists of the brain as Holger Hyden. At his laboratory in Göteborg, Sweden, Hyden has devised exquisite techniques for measuring the RNA in a single neuron. He has shown that, in brain areas where a great deal of learning occurs in a short period, there is an explosive increase of RNA. When the amount of RNA and protein increases inside the neuron, it decreases in the neuroglia outside. "It could be," Dr. Adey proposes, "that the electrical activity coursing through the neuroglia causes it to pour something into the fluid around the neuron that in turn alters the RNA and the protein inside the neuron."

Experiments conducted by Adey's team suggest that it takes about twenty minutes to change the firing pattern of a neuron. Biochemists say that is about the time needed to make any basic change in RNA. Twenty minutes is also approximately how long it takes for the memory to become permanent. Electroshock treatment wipes out remembrance of anything that happened during the twenty or so minutes prior to the shock. All earlier memories—safely deposited in the protein of the neurons—are retained in the storehouse of memory.

Dr. Adey's concept of the brain is one of many. Each researcher in this field proceeds with his own model—explicit or implicit—in mind. At present, there's no way of proving which one is "right"; the brain is far too complex for that. But some of Adey's key points are beginning to gain support in other labs. Dr. Phillip G. Nelson at the National Institute of Health has shown that the nerve cells in the spinal cord interact, not only by firing bursts from one to the other, but also on the basis of the more subtle electrical fields they themselves generate. The cells in the spinal cord are larger and more widely spaced than those in the brain. If they can transcend the "fire or no-fire" mode of operation, it makes it seem almost inevitable that cells tightly packed in the brain can do the same and more.

The complicated new math used by Dr. Adey and his colleagues in analyzing brain-wave activity finds affirmation in the work of Mr. Harry Blum of the Air Force Cambridge Research Laboratories. Mr. Blum writes that, "despite more than two millennia of geometry, no formulation which appears natural for the biological problem has emerged," and he goes on to seek new ways to describe shapes by analyzing waves of light that bounce off them. Similarly, Dr. Adey's team uses waves of electricity to describe events within the neurons in the brain. Research that tends to bolster Dr. Adey's theories also is being carried out in the laboratories of Otto D. Creutzfeldt in Germany and Yasuichiro Fujita and Toshio Sato in Japan.

If subtle electrical fields generated in the brain can affect thinking and perceiving, what would happen if the same sort of fields were applied from outside? Dr. James Hamer of Northrop Systems Laboratories has attempted to answer this question in a rigorously controlled series of experiments. Dr. Hamer applies low-voltage alternating current (only two volts) to aluminum plates on either side of human subjects' heads. The plates do not touch the head and the amount of electricity that can penetrate to the neurons is minuscule indeed—certainly not enough to set off neuronal firing. And yet, this tiny electric field significantly alters the subjects' perception of time.

All of which adds up to a sensitive and subtle brain indeed. With enough poetic license, we may view each of its neurons not merely as a computer-like cell with a single function, but as a versatile, complex personality in miniature. It may have a specialty, but is also able to participate in a multitude of memories, moods, perceptions and actions. It interacts directly with its neighbors, but also tunes in to news of distant events in the brain, ready to add its vote or its influence when the moment is appropriate. It has a stable, recognizable character, but is willing and able to change, to learn from experience.

A brain composed of such neurons obviously can never be "filled up." Perhaps the more it knows the more it *can* know and create. Perhaps, in fact, we can now propose an incredible hypothesis: *The ultimate creative capacity of the brain may be, for all practical purposes, infinite.*

But *how* are the capabilities of this marvelous organ to be tapped? And for whose benefit? The men who probe for the secrets of the central nervous system often find themselves asking these questions. Most of them assume that a better understanding of the brain will guarantee new techniques for achieving the human potential. But they grow cautious when asked for specific—if speculative —examples.

Not so cautious are some popular books and magazines. Stretching the substance of brain experiments to the shape of science fiction, they come up with futuristic thinking caps that will teach you, in a twinkling, everything there is to know about, say, calculus. Or intercranial hookups that will make it possible for students to get a famous professor's insights without the bother of listening to his lectures. From the speculation come two fairly promising tools for changing human behavior: electrical stimulation of the brain and mind-altering drugs.

As far back as 1936, the Canadian neurosurgeon Dr. Wilder Penfield discovered that electrical stimulation of certain brain areas (especially in the brains of epileptics) sometimes creates a vivid mental experience. The patient seems to be reliving old memories with one part of the mind while retaining consciousness of the present with another. Several researchers also have discovered that electrical current applied through slim electrodes inserted deep inside the brain of animals may strongly influence their actions.

Scientists at the Max Planck Institute at Seewiesen, Germany, for example, have probed for controlling centers in the brains of chickens. They never know exactly what action they will get from these small-brained creatures when they turn the current on. Electricity directed to one point may make the chicken into a compulsive eater. Applied a millimeter away, the electronic persuader may keep the chicken from eating at all. A little jolt in the rage center may cause a cock to beat his wings and clack his spurs against a stuffed animal.

The Planck Institute scientists moved closer to creating automatic chickens when they equipped them with tiny transistor radio receivers so that current could be turned on from a distance. This led to interesting social situations among a freely moving but transistorized flock of chickens. The low hen on the pecking order, the most chicken of the flock, could be turned into a tiger if her aggression center was stimulated.

Sometimes more than one electrode was activated within the chicken's brain, giving the scientists control over possibly contradictory behavior. One chicken, equipped with two electrodes, could be ordered electronically either to sit or to jump and flee. The scientists complicated things by turning on both the "sit" and the "jump" electrode at the same time. Confronted with a dilemma not unknown in ordinary human life, the chicken did the best she could. After a period of agitated shuffling, she sat down, remained seated for a while, then leaped up with a squawk.

A number of researchers in various parts of the world have carried on similar experiments with various animals. Dr. José Delgado of Yale's School of Medicine implanted a radio-controlled electrode in the fear center of a fighting bull; then, to prove his point, entered the bull ring. When the bull charged, Dr. Delgado pressed a button on a small transmitter he was carrying. The bull braked and backed off. Pictures of the episode appeared in the world press.

The finding that has most delighted the human imagination has to do with a deep-seated pleasure center. Dr. James Olds, then of McGill University in Montreal, discovered this wellspring of Elysium in the brain of a white rat in 1954. The rat, presented with a pedal attached to the electrode stuck in his own pleasure center, would spend most of his days and nights stimulating himself, oblivious to fine food and a lady rat alike.

In later experiments by Olds and others, rats have been known to press their pleasure pedals up to 8,000 times an hour and to carry on their electronic pursuit of happiness for weeks. What happens to these pleasure-bent rats? Do they, like some portrait of a rodent Dorian Gray, turn ravaged and worn? Bad news for the Puritans who linger among us: the orgiast rats generally end up in better physical and mental shape than do their pleasure-deprived littermates. They are alert. Their coats are glossy. Their eyes shine.

Pleasure centers of one sort or the other have been discovered in many animals, including cats, dogs, monkeys, dolphins and—perhaps—man himself. That this point is debatable may be illustrated by a possibly apocryphal account of what happened when a famous Scandinavian brain researcher (as an adjunct of therapy, of course) hit upon what he took to be the pleasure center in the brain of a male patient. Overjoyed, he phoned an American colleague, who took the first transoceanic jet to see for himself. When the American arrived on the scene, the patient was happily and repeatedly pressing a lever that sent a current through a wire into the electrode implanted in his brain. The American watched for a while, then asked permission to make just one little check. Permission granted, he went into the control rooms and disconnected the wire. The patient, not missing a beat, continued pressing the lever—enjoying, so he said, the same ecstatic sensation.

As we shall see later, this simple story has profound implications. It suggests that man may not *need* to be wired for joy—or for anything else. Over the ages, the human race has developed many ways for arriving at sensations that spring (as all do) from brain activity. It may be that anything a jolt of electricity can do, the activity we have defined as education can do even better.

Then, too, it is easy to weave scenarios of horror by taking brain probing to a totalitarian extreme: A brave new generalissimo of 1984 forms an electronically controlled army. Each soldier carries a little transistor receiver at the base of his skull from which electrodes run to various control points within the brain. Time for a long march? The generalissimo at his transmitter merely has to push the MARCH TIRELESSLY button. Time for rest and recuperation? SLEEP DEEPLY is the button to press. The enemy approaches. FIGHT FEARLESSLY does the trick. To the satirists of the future (if satire can survive science) we may leave the uses of the FORAGE button or that final one marked RAPE, PILLAGE AND DESTROY.

More sanguine scenarists have envisaged the electrical invasion of the skull in the service of knowledge and joy. What if scientists could get *enough* circuitry into the brain? Wouldn't it be possible then to deposit knowledge electronically? And what about using the pleasure center? Wouldn't that be a powerful reward for shaping desired behavior? (The properly wired student might get a jolt of pleasure rather than an "A" for spelling "serendipity" correctly.)

What credence should we give these fantasies? Since the birth of modern science, history has been unkind to most scoffers. A writer debunks even the wildest-sounding scientific speculation only at his own risk. Still, it must be said that most scenarists of electrical stimulation have been naïve or poorly informed. Against the marvelous intricacy of the human brain, the present brand of electrical stimulation appears a blunt instrument indeed. Thus far, it has been hard to handle, erratic and unreliable. The same electrode that once caused an animal to overeat may eventually cause exactly the opposite effect. Experiments by Elliot and Thelma Valenstein and others show that even the pleasure center has been oversold. A rat, it turns out, will keep switching an electric current on and off when it is applied at many different parts of his brain. There is no single, localized wellspring of joy.

A far more fundamental objection to electrical stimulation has been largely overlooked. UCLA's H. W. Magoun, an elder statesman among brain researchers, explained it to me: "Electrical implantation is a way of simulating what happens naturally. It is a rather crude prosthesis. But we don't need a crutch to get around if we have our legs. In our sense organs—eyes, ears and so on—we possess the most beautifully controlled, delicate and effective access to the brain. If we want to change a brain, we can best do it through our natural senses. That is what we *are* doing every day, what society has always done. The puzzle for the future is how to do it better."

Again, we are confronted with the environment, the stuff of education itself, as the most powerful instrument for achieving a greater use of our potentialities. But before looking into new "natural" methods that can expand human capabilities, we might briefly view one more "artificial" method: the use of drugs.

Chemistry, perhaps even more decisively than electricity, controls what goes on in the brain. Since before the beginnings of civilization, societies have conducted massive and generally quite effective chemical experiments with uninhibitors (alcohol), stimulants (caffeine), euphorics (marijuana), depressants (opium) and many other brain-changing substances.

Modern science has speeded the search for happiness and wisdom by the drink or the pill. Tranquilizers and psychic energizers already have revolutionized institutional care for the mentally ill, supplanting shock treatment and locked wards, calming the manic and cheering the depressed. Beyond therapy, these benign drugs—as the less benign side effects are refined away—may increasingly help the normal neurotic achieve more of his potential by putting him in the proper state to learn or act.

The search for chemical educators will go on. Already, researchers are administering drugs high in RNA to older people to find out if their memories can be improved; experimenters at Abbott Laboratories have developed and marketed a drug that appears to increase brain RNA. Another brain function that may be improved by drugs is the ability to focus attention, to filter out stimuli that experience has shown to be unimportant. The attention mechanism is thought to dwell in an area deep within the brainstem called the "reticular formation." Perhaps the psychic energizers act directly upon this area of the brain. A worldwide search is presently underway for a specific and effective "attention pill," a drug that will sharply and safely increase one's ability to give long and intense attention when desired.

The controversial hallucinogens, or psychedelics—notably LSD—have been used to create unfamiliar shifts in the condition of consciousness itself. These chemicals are currently under attack for their possibly dangerous side effects and for the youthful, dissident cultures that have grown up around their use. But, whatever the side effects, whatever the misuse among young people, the fact remains that hundreds of thousands of serious, mature people of all ages have used the drugs neither for kicks nor for therapy, but to gain glimpses of new and rich worlds of consciousness. To stand outside the standardized consciousness and perceptions of the immediate past, as will be seen later, becomes a matter of great importance during times of fast technological and cultural change. The psychedelics have provided quick journeys into other lands of the mind; they have expanded many people's concept of the possible. Even here, however, it is becoming clear that the kind of psychic mobility rudely thrust upon one by the psychedelics can be learned with no drugs whatever.

In fact, just as chemicals can change people's actions, so people's actions—their relationship with the environment, their education—can change their brain chemistry. How this works is being demonstrated in experiments at the University of California at Berkeley. For several years there, psychologist David Krech and his associates have been rearing matched sets of rats in two sharply contrasting environments. One set of rats lives in a sealed room. Each animal is isolated in a separate cage, in darkness and silence. Each is deprived of relationships with other rats or people. The second set of rats, littermates of the first, is kept in a rich and varied environment. They live together in large cages filled with playthings. They learn to explore mazes. They are taken out and handled every day.

Here is what Krech and his associates have discovered: Starting out the same at birth, the enriched rats develop a higher concentration of an important brain enzyme than do the deprived rats. Not only that; the size and weight of their brain cortex (the outer bark, associated with higher learning) becomes larger and heavier, because of the life they have lived. The deprived rats, when tested for learning ability, are far outperformed by their more richly educated littermates. They are mentally crippled.

One glimpse of that darkened room with its isolated and silent rats has come back to me many times—whenever I hear talk of "cultural deprivation" or visit a tenement in a big-city ghetto; whenever I go into any classroom where children are quelled, silenced, placed in rigid psychic isolation. Are these children being robbed of their potential brain tissue? If so, is there any worse crime?

But if the environment can take away, it can also enrich. Already, we find ordinary individuals performing feats that, in terms of past expectations, would be considered miraculous. Run-of-the-mill technicians today perform feats of abstract reasoning that would have a Pythagoras exclaiming in wonder. And what young daredevil of the early 1900s would have believed anyone who told him that, within his lifetime, hordes of housewives would be driving superpowered vehicles along four-lane raceways, scant feet apart, at better than a mile a minute? In those days, it was thought only supermen could ever perform such a feat. From this vantage point, we can say they were "wrong." But what well-established, commonly agreed-upon human limitation of today will we be "wrong" about tomorrow? In a sense, we might say that those freeway housewives *are* miraculous.

Brain Research Institute researchers have compared the brain-wave patterns of subjects driving along the Los Angeles freeways with those of jet pilots flying practice air-defense interception missions. The automobile drivers showed up with more complex and stressful patterns. And there are millions of them. As a matter of fact, mankind's universal response to the motorcar provides a good example of human potential and how it is best elicited. The automobile makes a perfect teacher. It is a highly interactive learning environment, providing quick feedback for the student driver's every action. Anything that can be verbalized by an instructor about this process is trivial compared with what the car in motion tells the learner. The interaction between environment (car in motion) and learner is frequent, intense and often novel. The learner's behavior is changed during the process. And, at best, learning to drive is ecstatic. (Ask any sixteen-year-old.) Little wonder, then, that practically every human on the planet can become in this respect—when we stand back and apprehend the miracle for what it is—a superman.

Not all environments are significantly interactive. The average lecture room, for example, is extremely low in interaction. No great amount of human potential is likely to be elicited there, and it is significant that college lecturers are sometimes among those who stress human limitations. One of history's more notable misapplications of environment as a change agent came during the 1920s and 1930s. That was when reformers were convinced all we had to do was provide the poor with clean housing as well as a decent wage and then sit back and wait for literature and the arts to flower. It was disappointment that flowered, however, and the cynics have had a good time ever since citing the model towns in England where poor miners used their new bathtubs to store coal. This is supposed to illustrate some ancient wisdom about "human nature." All it really illustrates, though, is that simply moving people from one kind of housing to another and giving them more money is *not* giving them the kind of environment that will educate, that is, *change* them.

This society is still plagued by the unexamined notion that placing the organism and the environment in physical proximity will somehow change the organism (and probably *not* change the environment). How many "culturally deprived" children have been taken in tow by well-meaning educators or clubwomen and led to art museums and symphony rehearsals? Have you seen those children as they move, straggling, whispering and nudging each other, from the Expressionist collection to the Colonial silverwork? There are still people who assume that, if slum children could just be "exposed" to enough "culture" in this manner, they would become polite, dress properly, quit dropping out of school and, in short, behave in such a way as to stop bothering us. No need to dwell on the enormous arrogance behind the assumption that "culture" as safely deposited in our museums is *better* than life on the streets. It is enough to say that such juxtaposition does not educate.

No environment can strongly affect a person unless it is strongly interactive. To be interactive, the environment must be responsive, that is, must provide relevant feedback to the learner. For the feedback to be relevant, it must meet the learner *where he is,* then program (that is, change in appropriate steps at appropriate times) as he changes. The learner changes (that is, is educated) through his responses to the environment.

Within these constraints, the human organism is incredibly flexible. If there are limits on the human ability to respond to learning environments, we are so far away from the limits as to make them presently inconsequential. Throughout human history to date, it has been the environments, not the human beings, that have run up against limitations. Now, for the first time, mankind has gained the physical, technological ability to create almost any kind of environment he can imagine. The situation may be difficult to comprehend, but it has, nonetheless, come to pass. We are now capable—without brain machines, without drugs, without eugenics—of educating people so that, not the few, but the many would appear to our present perceptions as geniuses of thinking, perceiving, feeling and being.

In this business of putting together the new environments that would bring forth the latent genius of man, we have arrived perhaps at the level of the invention of the wheel. Still, evidence is mounting to support the case for an almost limitless human potential. The evidence tells us, in answer to one of the questions that opened this chapter, that even moderate efforts, properly directed, may yield great gains.

The efforts that currently show the most promise move on two main frontiers that now are separate and often hostile, but may eventually merge into one. The first is rigorously scientific; the second may appear to threaten the scientific-rationalist outlook. The men on both frontiers, like the brain researchers, live in a state of high excitement, buoyed by good results almost everywhere they turn.

The man who argues most vehemently for the application of science to human affairs is Harvard University's controversial psychologist Professor B. F. Skinner. In recent years, many who have written about man's prospects in a technological future have attacked Skinner as the most diabolical architect of a dehumanized world. And yet, in one of those paradoxes which often accompany great turning points in history, it is Skinner and his followers who at this moment in time offer clear proof that the human potential outruns all our previous expectations.

To the popular mind, Professor Skinner is best known as the man who invented the teaching machine, who trained pigeons to play ping-pong and to guide a missile, who built an air-conditioned box in which to rear his baby and who wrote *Walden Two,* a novel about a rather dull utopia where behavioral techniques are used to achieve pastoral, nineteenth-century ideas of happiness and community. None of this suggests the importance of his work.

Professor Skinner himself may eventually find it paradoxical that his discoveries and techniques can be used to reach far more varied and ambitious goals than those envisaged in *Walden Two.* In any case, Skinner's clear and concise way of looking at the relationship between the organism and the environment may prove exceedingly useful to *anyone* interested in a thoroughgoing reform of education, whatever way that reform would move. Essentially, what he has done is strip the behavior of living things down to the bare bones, cutting straight through the verbiage, the dense theories, the "explanatory fictions"—to use his term—that have sometimes made psychology more a literary metaphor or an occult parlor game than a science, and that have sometimes blocked the way to human improvement. In a series of experiments with rats back in the 1930s (since corroborated with other animals, including man), he found a way to predict, measure and control the actions of living things, in some cases with nearly the precision of a physicist dealing with matter and energy. He reported on the experiments in *Behavior of Organisms* in 1938, a book that was politely ignored for more than fifteen years. During this period, Skinner carried his experiments forward, expanding them to include human behavior, debated anybody anywhere about his work and never wavered for a moment in his view that all behavior must be ultimately predictable, controllable and, therefore, improvable.

In 1954, he devised the idea of the modern teaching machine or programmed instruction, an application of his animal methods to people. Soon human beings were displaying the dramatic increase in learning rate previously seen only in Skinner's rats and pigeons. Since then, interest in (and attacks on) Skinnerian psychology have soared, and today a growing arena of psychology is inhabited by the men and women who would apply and expand his methods.

In the twilight of the Freudian age, when every housewife has been led to believe that human behavior is invariably more complex than it seems, Skinner's ideas sound startlingly simple and commonsensical. Unlike Freud, Skinner does not find that people are driven by mysterious inner forces that war with society. Unlike Pavlov, he does not find that people are slaves to things happening immediately around them. Unlike many modern psychologists, he deals, not in hypotheses and complex statistics, but in direct observation, prediction and control of behavior.

According to Skinner, your tendency toward any action —your "character," "personality," "motivation"—has been shaped mostly by the *consequences* of your past actions. How you will act in the future will be further shaped by *what happens* to you *after* any of your present or future actions—i.e., by your interactions with your environment. A baby's ability and tendency to say "mama" is developed, not so much by his parents *telling* him to "say mama," as by the smile or the attention he gets—i.e., *what happens*— when he does successfully voice the word. If the child never received any response whatsoever for saying "mama," he would very soon stop saying it. (Skinner calls this "extinction.") The baby would also stop saying it if punished for doing so, but then he would tend to fear and avoid whoever punished him.

Skinner has found that, not punishment, but reward—or, in his terms, "positive reinforcement"—is the most effective force for shaping or teaching. Positive reinforcement may turn out to be food, money, praise, a kiss, a smile, a fleeting nod of approval. Best of all, it may consist simply of getting a right answer and knowing it's right, of working out a puzzle, of mastering a skill, of finding new beauty and order in words, music, color. Every culture and subculture, every school, every home has its own way—acknowledged or unacknowledged—of using rewards and punishments. Too often, according to Skinner, people have relied on punishment or the threat of punishment to control other people. Or they have used gross and insulting positive reinforcement, such as money meted out in a crude piece-work system. Skinner's scientific and humane impulses meet in his desire to substitute reward for punishment, to rely increasingly on the more subtle and "beautiful" forms of positive reinforcement.

To this end, he and his followers have created systematic programs to change behavior. A person generally changes his behavior, or learns, according to Skinner, in gradual steps. The manner and frequency in which he is reinforced for making these steps largely determines how well and how quickly he learns. There are many aspects of human behavior for which no effective reinforcement program has yet been worked out. But the results in those cases where the technique has been applied are frequently spectacular, especially in the treatment of "hopeless" schizophrenia, mental retardation, stuttering, juvenile delinquency and the like.

When Skinnerian methods were applied to education,

the nation began hearing of good students who finished a semester's work in, say, geometry in four or five days; and poor students who, for the first time, could comprehend material that previously had seemed unfathomable. So powerful—and potentially profitable—was programmed instruction that hastily formed commercial outfits began flooding the market with various forms of the new educational tool, much of low quality. Gradually, however, a startling fact began to come clear: even shoddy and boring programs sometimes worked as well as conventional schooling.

How about really first-rate programmed instruction? Some time ago Skinner predicted that students would learn twice as much in half the time as before. He turned out to be not quite right. Often they do better than that. In almost every case, good programming has proven its ability to speed and smooth the learning process for great numbers of students, leaving teachers freer than ever before to go beyond mere essentials, beyond group teaching.

Perhaps the best measure of how the new method can clear the way for greater use of human ability comes from its application to beginning reading, the most crucial skill presently taught in our schools. A programmed reading course developed by M. W. Sullivan and Associates already has helped several hundred thousand children learn to read at an average of better than double the usual progress. Some readers make such spectacular headway that worried teachers devise stratagems to slow them. Educators who are willing to give children their heads watch a number of them reading at fifth- or sixth-grade level by the end of first grade. The programs, unless misused, have produced hardly any nonreaders—a particularly interesting note in view of claims by some "reading experts" that up to thirty percent of children are afflicted with mysterious neurological reading defects. The defects, according to Dr. Sullivan, generally do not reside, inherent and inescapable, within the brain, but result from confusing learning environments—the usual classroom situation, for example.

In the new situation created by Sullivan, children learn with individual workbooks, move at their own pace, make written responses at each step and quickly check their responses against the "answer" provided in the program. Each program has been tried out and rewritten several times to make sure it is responsive to the kind of children who will be using it. Those sections which do not work during the trial sessions are rewritten until they do. Thus, the vast majority of children who use the program are assured of ninety-five percent right answers.

Undoubtedly, such a learning aid will soon be regarded as primitive. It is limited in that it teaches "right answers" and only one set of them at a time. "This is just the beginning," Dr. Sullivan told me. "We've just started to redesign a little piece of our environment—the part of it that reinforces us for learning to read. Here, as always, the human potential outruns our expectations. We have no idea whatsoever what the human animal can do in a properly designed environment."

The work thus far cited gives a hopeful prognosis of man's ability to function more effectively and happily in a somewhat familiar world, but does not venture to create radically new environments. More far-out proposals and experiments are being made by psychologists, philosophers and educators who seem, at first glance, to be radically opposed to the Skinnerians. Many of these men are grouped around the humanistic-psychology field. They hold a highly optimistic view of man and often use the phrase "human potential." They are perhaps more concerned with personal than with objective knowledge and frequently quote philosopher Michael Polanyi's credo that "we know more than we can tell." They are free-swinging rather than rigorously scientific and feel that the first big step we could take toward increasing human ability and happiness would be merely to remove the artificial societal restraints that now bind us.

The men and women along this frontier are informed by the writings and the spirit of Abraham Maslow and Carl Rogers. Dr. Maslow, a professor of psychology at Brandeis University and president of the American Psychological Association, hit upon an idea so utterly simple and so utterly brilliant that it set psychology on its head. Instead of studying neurotic or psychotic people, he studied people who are particularly happy and successful. Instead of looking into the low points of mental illness, he examined the high points of human joy. The picture of humanity that emerged from these studies contrasted sharply with those drawn by the traditional psychologies. In "self-actualizing" people (Maslow's term for the happy ones) the personality splits and inner conflicts of "human nature" just did not exist. At first it was hard for Maslow to accept his own findings. "It has involved for me," he writes, "the continuous destruction of cherished axioms, the perpetual coping with seeming paradoxes, contradictions and vaguenesses, and the occasional collapse around my ears of long-established, firmly believed-in and seemingly unassailable laws of psychology. Often, these have turned out to be no laws at all but only rules for living in a state of mild and chronic psychopathology and fearfulness, of stunting and crippling and immaturity which we don't notice because most others have this same disease we have."

Maslow could not escape the consequences of his findings. The old laws would have to collapse. Theories based on the needs and strivings of deprived people might be appropriate to a depriving world. But they do not define man's "nature" or speak to the human potential. The self-actualizing people are not theoretical. They exist all around us. By turning our attention—and our expectations —toward them, we step easily across barriers once considered fixed and final. And Maslow, describing the self-actualized, provides clues in our search for expanded human capacity. He gropes for words, lists "characteristics of the healthy human specimen" (more openness to experience, increased integration, increased spontaneity, etc.), but always comes back to one theme: the self-actualizers are somehow both mature and childlike. They manifest what he calls "healthy childishness" and "a second naïveté."

Like Maslow, Dr. Carl Rogers, now a senior fellow at the Western Behavioral Sciences Institute, is possessed by a fierce faith in the human potential. This faith flowed into his development of Client-Centered Therapy. Here, the client (not "patient") defines and seeks his own goals; the therapist serves merely as a "facilitator" toward them. Client-Centered Therapy is vulnerable to parody: the therapist always seems to be repeating the client's words, or simply saying, "M-hm." But even parody affirms Rogers' unshakable theme, repeated in many ways over many years: *It has been my experience that persons have a basically positive direction.*

Both Maslow and Rogers are now interested in the "intensive small-group experience." In these experiences, people gather in groups of around seven to fifteen. They use a whole spectrum of techniques to break old patterns of relating, to expand their sensory and emotional range and, simply, to achieve joy. There are many varieties of these groups and many names for them, including "T-Groups" (from the early work of the National Training

Laboratory in Bethel, Maine), "sensitivity-training groups" and "encounter groups."

In the simplest kind of encounter groups, people learn to change their modes of relating and expressing themselves in a surprisingly short time. Formal, verbal instructions can be few: "Be completely open and honest, relate on the level of feelings rather than rationalizations and stay in the here and now rather than the past or future." Starting with this and moving through a series of practice techniques, most people find it possible to drop the old masks, the defenses, the deviousness that have cut them off from their own feelings and from the ability to express them to others. Hardened executives often end up revealing more of their deepest, most carefully guarded secrets to members of their group than they have ever revealed to their own wives, friends, brothers. Some shed tears of sadness over the essential loneliness of their lives; others weep with relief and joy of being able to let go of long-repressed hostility or anxiety. Most find that this new openness allows them ultimately to be more effective on the job, with their friends and families. It is significant that business and industry—especially the aerospace industry—sponsor a large share of these groups. Many management theorists believe that the usual efforts to scheme, manipulate and disguise true feelings waste better than fifty percent of the average executive's energy and time. Then, too, the intricate task of creating a spacecraft requires far more trust, candor and sensitivity than did the old production line. Corporations pursue an expanded human ability to express feelings and relate with others, not for altruism's sake, but for higher profits.

None of this, it might be noted, is "therapy," and only confusion will follow from viewing it as such. It is practical-minded preparation for living in a world of unprecedented flux. In his recent book, *Joy,* Dr. William Schutz of Esalen Institute presents forty of the new techniques for achieving a fuller development of human potential. The techniques range from expressive body movements through fantasy to verbal confrontation. Most of them start with the basic encounter group. Most can be practiced without the help of professional therapists. The success that Dr. Schutz, other pioneering professionals and laymen are achieving with an ever-expanding spectrum of techniques suggests that a new domain of learning already is available to educators at every level.

All of this doubtlessly will soon seem timid. It is likely that human capabilities will be most significantly stretched in new, man-made environments and reinforcement systems that would be hard for us to imagine. To move toward them means breaking free of "doctrines," "movements" and "schools of thought"—those old enemies of human development. A new generation of researchers (some of whom will be discussed in later chapters) is prepared to draw from Skinner's work or from the humanists' or from anyone else's; to use programmed reinforcement along with encounter groups; to pursue the human potential wherever it leads, even if it be toward what is now termed "psychic" or "mystical," even if it be called "fantastic." A few steps in that direction already are being taken.

For example, Dr. Joe Kamiya of San Francisco's Langley Porter Neuropsychiatric Clinic, using the simplest reinforcement techniques, is among those who are now teaching people to control such "inner" states as their basic brain-wave patterns. In his brain-wave experiments, Dr. Kamiya has his subjects lie in a quiet room, eyes closed, with electrodes attached to their scalps. He tells them only that, when they are "right," a tone will sound. The apparatus is hooked up so that, if Dr. Kamiya wants the subjects to increase a particular brain wave, the appearance of that wave will automatically set off the tone. (A similar technique decreases brain waves or blood pressure.)

At first the tone sounds only when, more or less by accident, the desired wave form appears. Merely by reacting to the reinforcement of the tone, the subjects gradually learn to make it sound more frequently and thus to increase the desired brain wave. When they learn to enhance the alpha-wave pattern, subjects tell of reaching a state of heightened awareness. They become relaxed, but not drowsy. They arrive finally at a state they term "serene." Dr. J. T. Hart of the University of California at Irvine, another researcher who works on the control of brain waves, has predicted that some day people may use the technique to turn off anxiety without drugs.

But there is a more profound hope in this research. According to recent studies in Japan, the people taking part in brain-wave experiments are accomplishing at least a part of the inner control that yogis and Zen Masters achieve only after many years of the most severe and selfless discipline. Many of *Dr. Kamiya's subjects achieve it in about twelve one-hour sessions*. "These experiments," Dr. Kamiya said, "suggest that eventually we shall find ways of influencing for the better almost every aspect of the life of man."

head of UCLA's Biotechnology Laboratory has announced, a bit apologetically, that it may take as long as a hundred years or more before teleportation comes to be. In teleportation, according to Dr. John Lyman, a man's entire genetic code would be fed to a computer, flashed to a receiving computer on the moon or a planet, and instantly reconstructed into the person who stood on earth a few seconds earlier. "Teleportation is still pretty wild stuff," Dr. Lyman was quoted as saying, "but the basic concept does not violate any known physical laws."

But extrapolation, no matter how bold, is only a way of measuring and stating present perceptions. To deal with the future, we must perceive the unperceived, the naked environment itself. Marshall McLuhan has said he couldn't tell you who discovered water, but it was certainly not the fish. And yet water is the fish's master mentor, determining his way of moving, his very shape, his cool, wet ecstasy. How can we discover the waters that surround man, the unseen teachers that shape our being? Let us question the unquestioned, then ask how much of the naked environment can, after all, be manipulated to further the education of mankind.

From before birth, all humans are caressed and threatened by the affinity of matter to matter, the graceful warp in space we know as gravity. The newborn baby, according to behaviorists, fears only two things: a sudden noise or a sudden loosening of the embrace gravity provides between itself and the object supporting it, i.e., the sensation of falling. Throughout life, gravity in interplay with inertia and movement is a powerful and pervasive teacher, giving us subtle, finely graded feedback for a great variety of learning. It teaches us through both positive and negative reinforcement, and the ratio between the two (with positive highly predominant over negative under the usual earthbound conditions) could well serve as an optimum model for many less pervasive, more specialized educators —schoolteachers, for example.

Only when we at last step beyond gravity do we realize how powerfully it has taught us. The first space-walking astronauts found themselves unable to perform the simplest physical tasks without the accustomed guidance of their most constant tutor. But learned behavior is reversible. Once space technicians set about creating a systematic learning program, including new gadgets, for getting along without gravity, astronauts began performing adequately in a new environment.

The naked environment teaches, shapes and aids us everywhere. But it also limits. The simple properties of the phenomenon we call light serve as a sort of straight-edge against which we may plot the plans for our perceptions and actions. Light has often seemed, with its great speed and copious information-carrying qualities, the royal band of the energy spectrum. It was only with the invention of the laser that we began to question the limitations of those onrushing, incoherent, strictly linear, ricocheting photons that we have thus far dealt with. Now, it appears, lasers and other devices can help us create far more sophisticated forms of light that can carry vastly more information and thereby provide for us vastly increased feedback. When and if new light environments become pervasive enough, we ourselves will change.

What does all this have to do with education? More than we might realize. Taking the naked environment for granted, we fail to realize that seeing itself is, in part, learned behavior. When a person blind from birth suddenly gains access to light, he hardly *sees* at all. Generally he learns quickly enough, having a full arsenal of cues from the other senses and the verbal environment to aid him. Still, though he "knows" the difference between a square and a triangle perfectly well, it will be a long time before he can distinguish one from the other without stopping to count the sides.

Watch the new baby learn to see. Better say "see *and act*," for nothing is learned that is not somehow, in some manner, consequential. The baby lies on its back; a shining toy is held before it. When the eyes' random movements bring the object into the field of vision, *something happens*. Through chains of optic nerves, chemical balance swiftly shifts, electrical charges fire. Electrochemical activity pulses in, excites a large area of the occipital lobes of the brain, in the back of the baby's head. The whole brain responds to some extent, and there is even a perturbation in the overall, ongoing brain-wave pattern. All of this *something happening* is highly reinforcing, and when the baby's eyes wander away from the object, the reinforcement stops. Gradually, in small steps, in successive approximations, the baby learns to control the extrinsic eye muscles so as to keep the exciting object in the field of vision.

But that is only a beginning. The baby can increase the amount of reinforcing visual stimulation by focusing the lens, by fixing both eyes on the object with the proper convergence, by adjusting the size of the pupil to maximize the contrast between object and background in term of the retina's range of sensitivity. And then, of course, the baby goes on to coordinate vision with arm and hand movement (aided by gravity and inertia and kinesthesia as well as light) so as to reach up and take hold of a toy.

Such "natural" developments require interaction between the organism (baby) and the environment. If the properties of the environment were different, if gravity, light, inertia, air, sound and the like were not as they are, then learning would be different and the resulting organism, though clothed in a human body, would be different indeed.

All behavioral development is a function of learning. Some psychologists and physiologists have defined what may be termed "optimal" ages for given types of learning, as if these periods exist apart from the nature of the environment. They do indeed exist in any given environment. But they do not spring up purely from within the organism.

A human best learns to talk at age two because he has completed the necessary prior learning and has not yet come under the influence of other modes of reinforcement (athletic activity, for example) that would compete with the reinforcements in learning to talk. At that age in most present human cultures, the baby is surrounded by an ideal environment for precisely this type of learning. It is hard to teach a fifteen-year-old to talk, but probably not because his neurological system has mysteriously "grown" past some optimum point. Whatever kept the fifteen-year-old from learning to talk probably also got in the way of necessary prior learning. By fifteen, he has most likely come under the influence of competing satisfactions. And the learning environment we would provide him would most likely be wildly inappropriate; we might even try to "teach" him rather than being delightedly responsive to his free learning.

Learning to see, learning to talk, learning to love all take place in a Little Round Schoolhouse called Earth, replete with audiovisual aids that we are only just now realizing we can manipulate. "Natural enemies" have taught us well, have shaped our species. We are rapidly dismissing those useful old instructors and replacing them with educators of our own making.

And yet, many of the old teachers are still with us, especially those we never realized were teaching. For example, the human organism is educated—and limited—by the inexorable day-night cycle of a rotating planet. Here, again, we become aware of an environmental condition's power only when we start transcending it. Current research on what happens to those who jet east or west across several time zones only confirms what many travelers have suspected since the jetliners began to fly: interaction with the terrestrial twenty-four-hour cycle shapes many aspects of our being into resonant cycles. Functions that range from digestion to dreaming, from sex to sweating need recycling after a quick hop from New York to Teheran. We have yet to know precisely the diurnal or nocturnal patterns of hormonal and other systems. Perhaps breaking prior conditions of longitudinal place will help us better understand the human mechanism.

The unseen educators surround us. Not acknowledging their presence, we do their bidding. Words, for example, crowd our world, shape us, block our vision of the silent joys. Aldous Huxley once estimated that seventy percent of human existence is dominated by the verbal. We have learned how strikingly perceptions change when filtered through different languages, especially those of such peoples as the Hopi Indians. But what happens when we escape—if only for a time—from language itself? Experiments in Huxley's "nonverbal humanities" reveal the opulence of the existence that waits for us behind the screen of words.

The awakenings offered by fast technological change often are rude ones. Perhaps nothing prepares us so well for the shock of recognizing the naked environment as does science fiction. Robert Heinlein's *Stranger in a*

Strange Land is in this respect among the very best. The stranger is Michael Smith, an earthling of the future who was reared from birth in the very different and, in many ways, advanced environment of Mars. The genius of *Stranger* springs from the fact that the reader is not asked to watch someone like himself adapt to an imagined alien culture. Instead, he sees an earthman, free of our environmental limitations, attempt to adapt to conditions of life we commonly take for granted. This device makes such ordinary things as bipolar sexuality, inflexible time sense and aging and death seem quite extraordinary, as perhaps they are.

About sex, Heinlein wrote: "Martians and humans were both self-aware life forms but they had gone in vastly different directions. All human behavior, all human motivations, all man's hopes and fears, were colored and controlled by mankind's tragic and oddly beautiful pattern of reproduction." Heinlein's Martians, we are led to believe, had no conventional bipolar sexuality, but they did have a rich and ceremonial "growing closer." Michael Smith's attempts to understand human sexuality, his subsequent cross-cultural working out of new sexual patterns make the reader sharply aware of how our "natural" sexual constraints shape and limit us.

This may be fiction, but it is fiction informed by reality. Right here on earth, sexuality is now being separated from procreation. Just as the birth-control pill frees the sex act from reproduction, so sperm banks and artificial insemination free reproduction from the sex act. Against these new environmental conditions, young people already are working out new sexual patterns that sometimes seem as strange and threatening to the old as a Martian invasion.

On Heinlein's Mars, time has come under the control of consciousness as have the processes of aging and physical

death. Here on earth, we of the West have generally regarded time as a constant, a steadily flowing measure of all
events and of life itself. But now time's constancy is under
attack within our own civilization—conceptually in relativity physics, artistically in films, novels, poems, plays, and
personally in widespread time-altering experiments with
psychedelic drugs and other methods. Perhaps time is the
ultimate water in which we swim, and we shall never really
know what it is to be human until we are able to pull ourselves up on the bank of timelessness and view the scene
behind. This, in any case, has been a central theme of the
religious mystics, though when they return from the time-
less world they bring us often quite disparate instructions
of what to do with our lives in time.

Even the process of aging, it now appears, may be manipulated to some extent, and gerontologists are beginning to
question that there is any inevitable physiological necessity
for the cellular forgetting that leads to dissolution and
death.

We would have to be naïve indeed to suppose that such
crucial overthrows of basic human conditions could come
to pass without affecting the very foundations of mankind's
education and eventually creating a new kind of man.

How can we discover the naked environment, the givens
of the educational situation? There can be no final answer,
only a series of new questions stretching to the ends of our
perceptions and beyond. Start with the simplest: that we
are driven, shaped, educated by our constant needs for
food and water and salt (how many school principals will
show visitors the new cafeteria before showing a single
classroom?); that the stuff we consume takes such diverse
form, so ingeniously found, so brutally got (we devour
root, stem, leaf, seed, fruit, bark, peel; relish the liver of

baby bull; steal the food of bees); that periodically we must defecate the waste of all this devouring (a book could be written on the educational contingencies around "being excused"; the history of civilization might be traced in the history of plumbing); that we live on the floor of an air ocean in which other creatures fly, clouds soar, odors waft, heat hovers, sounds mingle; that we must keep bringing this air into our bodies, awake or asleep, every few minutes or die; that rains fall, rivers flow; that our bodies in water poise between sinking and floating while stone goes down and wood rises (imagine the history of man had the specific gravity of wood been a few points greater); that the ultimate source of all our energy is single, a ball of flaming gas ninety-three million miles away.

Another thing that profoundly affects our thinking and striving is the very fact that the environment has the capacity to provide forms of energy that our unaided senses at present do *not* perceive. If there were nothing at all that we could *not* sense, our lives and our expectations would be radically different. We would not be making the great turn toward technology involved in harnessing electromagnetic energy for radio, television, radar, X ray, radiotelescopy, computers and all of electronics.

The existence of unperceived and unharnessed forms of energy puts stretch in the human system; it stretches us not only toward an increasingly technological existence, but toward the vast, unknown realm that we call (pending the time we learn to manipulate each of its specifics) the "mystical."

The new question here becomes: What is the environmental potential? Will we find ourselves running out of unused environmental resources? Not likely. New subatomic particles, new quanta of energy are still being discovered. The neutrino, for example, is an elusive one, a particle particularly reluctant to interact. Ten billion of these tiny bits of energy from space can penetrate the entire bulk of the earth and come out the other side before a single one interacts in any way with anything in its path. But the neutrino is there for us to use when we can. What will be the neutrino's role in the education of the future?

Look deeper for the naked environment. Perceive differently. Perhaps the human body itself, as Michael Murphy of the Esalen Institute has suggested, can be viewed as environment. Perhaps we limit ourselves by considering our skin as the crucial boundary between the self and its world. The body has been educated by the environment, but at any present moment it is a prodigious producer of stimuli on its own, apart from the stimuli it receives from outside the skin. The muscles have ways of signaling their positions, movements, tension and tone. And there are messages from digestive, circulatory and sexual systems, from the delicately balanced hormonal circuits. When we of the West classify this activity as "involuntary," we reveal a failure of no small dimension; for ways do exist and have long been known in other cultures for bringing these "involuntary" bodily functions under voluntary control, and thus opening up a whole "new" environment for the benefit of the self.

Truly, Western civilization's neglect of the body is nothing less than scandalous, for it has made a rich universe of energy, action and information practically invisible. The body may also be thought of as an extension of the outer environment, for outside stimuli are processed, filtered, changed by it before they reach consciousness. Inner and outer are composed alike of matter and energy and possibilities. Seeing each as extensions of the other helps us perceive essential unity where multitudes of theoreticians have debated fruitlessly over modes of separateness. The body may act both as organism to the outer environment and as environment to the center of consciousness. Its possibilities in education are powerful indeed.

Or look at it another way. Theoretically, a varied and intense sensory life can be had without the body at all. As science writer Arthur C. Clarke has pointed out, all sensations are simply electrochemical activity in the brain. Therefore, if there were a way of hooking the disembodied brain to enough artificial sensors (including surrogate body sensors), then this brain could enjoy all the conscious sensations of normal life and more. If the sensors could be joined to a worldwide network, the brain could "be" anywhere on earth in a twinkling, "feeling" and "seeing" and engaging in almost unlimited sensory behavior. In this light, embodiment itself appears as a limitation. Having to move an old-fashioned body into physical proximity to another sentient being in order to converse or make love seems crude and ponderous indeed.

Some aspects of this worldwide sensory mobility already are available with the TV communications satellite, and the personal and societal effects of instantaneous vision and hearing on a global scale are yet to be imagined.

Nor is disembodiment required for the senses to suffer a sea change into something rich and strange. When Jacques-Yves Cousteau devised the aqualung, he was not so much a pioneer of a silent world as an alchemist of the perceptions. For to enter that dim and dreamlike realm, where colors are somehow more vivid and all things eerily near, is to abandon your senses of time and place and motion. Cooled, silenced, encompassed—in that very yielding, the being itself may burst from the body's familiar prison. This truly is metamorphosis, the ancient magical myth suddenly come true: man into fish, freer of the surface than dolphin or whale.

Even more triumphantly free is the skydiver. Buoyed up only by the hundred-mile-an-hour race of invisible air, he plays tricks with gravity and ancestral fears. The earth seems far below; the diver seems suspended in space. Time is altered in that long skyborne interval until a half minute seems half a lifetime. Nor does the diver simply plummet. He draws back his arms, tilting his body forward against the uprushing tide of air; he moves horizontally over the face of the earth just as fast as he approaches it. Quick as the wish, he may turn and glide toward a fellow diver. And if he can catch a flying girl, he may grasp her arms and share a perilous kiss, saved from certain death by his willingness and ability to break the embrace.

Only the earthbound could call sky merely blue or clouds merely white and gray. Flying through one of those glistening, cloud-bordered countries of the upper air, one redefines the whole notion of light and color. The most transparent, most swiftly shifting hue is somehow the most vivid. Near sunset, those colors deepen, and that is when the skydiver, godlike, can start high and bring the sun down with him, sinking into a huge pool of blue and purple dusk. For all of this he pays only the light tribute to mortality entailed in the requisite in-flight discipline and proper care of gear.

It is too bad that no poets have been skydivers and that no men of letters have orbited the earth. For one of the responsibilities of poetry and literature, if not to prepare us for the future, is at least to help us know the present. The poet might proclaim that his predecessors' fantasies already have come to pass, and he might go on to help us find new fantasies worthy of this age. The writer might tell us that, while environments limit, perceiving and changing environments liberates. He might even suggest that the most valuable by-products of space exploration will not be new consumer products but something infi-nitely more valuable: new perceptions.

And one of them might be so bold as to write, placing the words in quotes only to remind us that all language is incomplete, approximate and metaphorical, "All things are possible."

ALL LIVING THINGS—paramecium, plant, person—learn through interaction with the environment. All behavior, including that commonly called "instinctive" or "species-specific," is learned. In the lower organisms it is learned not so much during the life of any individual of the species as during the life-span of the species itself. Standing back and viewing learning on a species-long scale, we can sense again the unity of all life.

4. THE CHAIN OF LEARNING

Learning involves memory, that is, the storage of information. Man's large, complex, yet unified central nervous system can store great amounts of new information during the individual's lifetime and can revamp information already stored. All the brain cells, as well as the material between the cells, have their own ways of responding to every contingency. These ways of responding, as we have seen, may be traced back to thin, chainlike molecules of RNA or DNA, which serve as tiny reference libraries, holding incredibly great amounts of coded information. The DNA, passed down from our ancestors, contains information about the brain cell's basic structure and composition (just as it does for all of the body's cells). The RNA serves as a messenger from the DNA and a template upon which the protein of the cell may build. During learning, the RNA also helps modify the brain cell's composition so as to *change* its way of behaving. It may be said that a record of our lifetime's learning is kept in those tiny, chainlike molecules.

A lower organism, with its small, relatively undeveloped central nervous system, has only a limited ability to learn (that is, change its behavior) during a single life-span. And yet, the species does change in the long run as its environment changes. It may change in what we call behavior alone or in physical form as well. The distinction, from a larger viewpoint, is not significant. The robin is a robin because it has a yellow bill twenty millimeters long. It is a robin just as much because it hunts earthworms in a stereotyped manner and builds a certain kind of nest at a certain kind of place at a certain time. In this sense, physical changes and behavioral changes are the same. Any deviation very far from the norm either in length of bill or in nesting and feeding habits would prove perilous in terms of "robinness"—and survival.

We call species-long learning "adaptation" or, when the species shifts in physical form so that *we* recognize it as something separate, "evolution." A record of these changes, this education, is kept in the DNA, the microscopic libraries of learning that are passed down from generation to generation. Whether in earthworm, robin or man, the chemical scheme, the language in the molecules, is the same. But the words and the length of the message are different. They tell a story of the species' victorious interaction with the environment. Each seed is a chronicle of success.

The record of all learning for all life is written on the same tablets. Learning can occur, not just during the life of a single organism, but in species-long spans, on a geological time scale. This species-long learning (without appeal to Lamarckism) exhibits all the characteristics of learning that have been described thus far.

The change in a species invariably results from interaction with environment. It relates to the frequency, variety and intensity of the interaction. Just as the baby, to learn to talk, needs a variety of sounds out of which the particular sounds useful to a given culture may be reinforced, so the species, to adapt or evolve, needs variety in its progeny so the behaviors and physical characteristics adaptive to a given environment may be reinforced by natural selection. Genetic differences, from minor variations to major mutations, provide the range.

And ecstasy? The crucial acts of learning in species-long education are the ecstatic moments of conception and death. The maladapted individual that dies before reproducing contributes to the education of the species just as does the individual that conceives and brings forth new life. It may be said that the species learns by dying, that is, by the death of certain of its individuals. Those which live,

live totally. Just as every seed is a chronicle of success, every animal, in the words of André Gide, is a parcel of joy.

The interaction between species and environment is invariably a two-way process. As the species flourishes or declines, it affects the ecological balance, changes the conditions of life for many other species—and for itself. Species have had to respond (with adaptation, evolution or extinction) to repeated geological convolutions that have created new climates, new mountains, new plains, new seas. And yet, the geological changes alone are not nearly enough to explain the wholesale extinction of whole families of life during certain crisis periods in the earth's long history. Only about a third of the 2,500 families of animals that have left fossil records still exist (though even more families have subsequently developed). A few became extinct by evolving into new families, but the majority disappeared without leaving descendants. Some of the great mass extinctions occurred at times when no geological cataclysm was under way. In fact, as paleontologist Norman D. Newell has pointed out, even a relatively minor geological change, say the drying out of tidal flats, can affect the fortunes of certain species. The subsequent effect on the ecological balance can be more cataclysmic than earthquakes and glacial slides.

The species *Homo sapiens* has proven to be an ecological catastrophe for all manner of life. The extinction in North America of such large mammals as the mammoth, the giant sloth, the camel and the mastodon between 11,000 and 6,000 years ago has been attributed usually to a sudden change in climate. The best recent evidence, however, suggests that the real cause was the arrival of well-armed hunting bands from Asia. But, again, just as man affected the environment, the consequences of his actions—the extinction of so many mammals—powerfully affected his subsequent condition. Life's interdependence is total. The chain of learning is endless.

Why do some species succeed in learning from their environments while others fail? For the same reason that your child succeeds or fails in school. Here we may borrow the terminology of programmed instruction. If the learning steps are too great, if the environment changes too fast, no learning (adaptation or evolution) can take place and the species may perish. In an extremely stable environment, on the other hand, the species may survive but change hardly at all. Even in a changing environment, certain species have learned ways to withdraw at critical periods, to suspend interaction and thus to increase their chances of surviving change. Consider some of the old ones, creatures that have weathered many crises in evolutionary history: the crocodile, the turtle, the opossum. There is a periodic sluggishness about them. Like those recalcitrant students who sit in the rearmost seats, they can pull back into a stuporous immobility whenever real learning threatens. Most slow learners on the evolutionary scene, however, have no such defenses. They simply bow out when the teacher unexpectedly steps up the tempo of the lessons. No need for obscure and unsupported hypotheses about "the exhaustion of germ plasma" to account for evolutionary dropouts.

On the other hand, some learning feats of even the simpleminded creatures seem incredible. The operating principles of programming may help make them understood. The green turtle in certain South Atlantic colonies, for example, navigates 1,400 miles without a landmark, from Brazil to Ascension Island, a tiny dot on the open ocean. The feat in itself argues (though by no means proves) that Ascension is the last outcropping of what once was a vaster land mass. Perhaps when the green turtle first evolved, the Great Atlantic Ridge, now sunken, humped a thousand-mile-long spine out of the sea, making a target nearly impossible to miss. As the ridge gradually disappeared beneath the water, generations of green turtles gradually learned finer and finer positional discrimination.

What sensors did they use? *This is really not the most important question,* since there are so many available: visual ability to fix the precise height of the sun at noon on any given day; magnetic sense; supersensitive olfactory capability that would make each ocean current as easy to read as a road map—or perhaps some ability to sense a source of energy we know nothing about. A more important question is the schedule of the learning, the tempo at which the land mass shrinks against the rate at which the species can learn by evolutionary selection.

This gradual, programmed withdrawal of behavioral cues is indeed a favorite conditioning stratagem, called "fading." If a student wishes to memorize a poem, for instance, he first reads it through. Then, with each successive reading, he erases a few words until, at last, all he needs is the words in the title to set off the behavior of reciting the entire poem. Using this technique, an unfettered learner can master a sonnet in a few minutes. A turtle species, however, may take a million generations, starting with, say, a gradually shrinking, thousand-mile-long land mass, in learning to navigate to an island five miles in diameter. In both cases, the programmed fading must not proceed too fast. The student would not start right out by erasing the last six lines of "The World Is Too Much With Us." And in both cases, the results—whether meditated by turtle DNA or brain RNA—will seem remarkable to us only because we have not yet fully realized the power of optimal education for *any* organism or species.

The lower animals exhibit inflexible, stereotyped responses, and this is indeed quite useful for them. Such responses allow creatures with extremely simple nervous systems to draw directly upon learning programs millions of years long. And it must be said that man has lost something in becoming cut off from species-specific or instinctive behavior, most particularly those behaviors regulating population and prohibiting killing within a species. Recent books on territoriality (a chief means of species population control) and aggression have been widely interpreted as linking man with the animal kingdom in instinctive matters. Actually the books provide striking examples of how man *differs* from all other earthly creatures in these behaviors.

There is no need to say that man has no instincts whatever. Obviously, he is limited to some extent by the experiences gained from a long ancestry in interaction with the earth environment. The very shape of his body (no wings, no fins), the very makeup of his endocrine system aim him in certain directions. But even in something as urgent as the sex drive, to take an example, man is notable for the multitude of changes he is capable of ringing. Instincts, if you wish, are present but, in comparison with those of other animals, are truly unremarkable.

The ancient learning of the species called man is passed down in the cleverly comprehensive code of the DNA molecules. A key message in the code for this species may be summarized as follows: "Construct now an organism that will do most of its learning during its individual lifetime." From this, the organism derives its very essence. All the other particularities that have been cited to distinguish man from animal—upright stance, opposable thumb, massive brain—may be viewed as means to this end. To achieve it, man has sacrificed almost all the stereotyped biological responses that rule the lives of the lower organisms. Man is not without his own automatic behaviors; from this vantage point, life would seem unbearably difficult if we approached each experience as if for the first time, responding always afresh. Our present automatic responses are passed down, however, not so much by DNA as by an agency that in some cases seems equally rigid and repetitive. That agency is society.

Social entities themselves interact with their environments in the process of change we have called education. In this process, they display, again, the learning characteristics previously outlined. Societal learning is far faster than species-long learning. Its permutations are many, transcending the simple survive-or-die mode of species learning, while retaining survival (of the society, not its individual members) as a final criterion. Social information-storage devices entirely bypass DNA. Many of them—epics, rituals, mores—preceded written records. During preliterate times, people undoubtedly performed routine tasks of memorization that would stun present-day memory experts. Indeed, Socrates questioned the introduction of a written alphabet as a threat to Memory, the guardian (it must then have seemed) of survival itself. But whether social learning is stored in song or on shelves, each human individual draws upon a learning program that goes back many centuries.

In these programs may be found the "nature" of man. All those writers who have delineated "human nature" (and note that the term itself has a pessimistic, limiting ring to it) have actually been writing about the nature of human societies. More specifically, they generally have been referring to societies since the Agricultural Revolution. That dramatic event dates back perhaps 15,000 years, when, in certain parts of the world, the Paleolithic Age gave way to the Neolithic; when, in the simplest terms, men stopped being free-roving hunters and took up the ways of farmers.

How can we fully comprehend the enormity of this event? Before agriculture, most people spent lives of total involvement. Man the hunter learned what was necessary from the tribal memory bank—the skills, the conventions, the minimal stereotyped responses—but did not then stop learning. Roving freely, interacting directly with his environment, the hunter went on learning, changing, all life long. He had no job except education, a fact noted by Thoreau when he pointed to the American Indian as the perfect lifelong learner. The hunter was firmly linked to a schedule of positive reinforcements—subtle, specific and precise. He planned, he maneuvered in concert with his fellows, he used all of his senses. He grew wise with age. The consequences of his acts were reasonably clear. There was little conflict between private impulse and the general good. No complex battery of punishments, artificially imposed by society, was necessary.

Perhaps this Noble Savage, rescued from romantic longings for lost innocence (whatever that is), can once again aid our educational quest. For it was as hunter that man became man. The magnificent human central nervous system—the most complex, the most disentropic entity in the known universe—was not developed in farmers, scribes, kings, cobblers, accountants or nuclear physicists. These specialists, indeed, have always served as components of a larger whole, a service that rarely has required the total range or reach of the human faculties brought into play during a single day of the hunter's life.

Modern archeological methods are now making it possible to reconstruct prehistorical hunts even down to such details as the month of the year in which they occurred, the wind direction, the weapons used. Recent diggings near the village of Torralba in Spain reveal that, even thousands of centuries ago, hunters were using fire to stampede elephants and rhinoceroses into a bog.

Little by little, the ancient moments come to life: the glitter of eyes around a campfire; talk that has the immediacy of poetry or food; the hunters with small clay cups of embers creeping around the elephant herd on a day when the wind is right; each hunter taking his place along a valley that leads to the trap, every sense alive and fully awake, totally aware of the total environment; the acrid, crackling fire and the great beasts running. The hunters of Torralba shout their joy to us across the centuries.

Man the hunter, superb in probing a natural environment, in manipulating the fully interlocking and self-regenerating system of the wilds, lacked only that which at last prevailed over him and made his progeny less whole than he: man-made environments.

When the hunter's children first built societies based on agriculture, two new things entered the human experience: specialization and long-delayed reward. Specialization at first was not extreme; men cooperated to perform what appear even now as miracles of plant domestication and animal breeding. From the very beginning, however, it must have been no easy matter to take arduous action (plowing and planting) in the spring, then wait several months for the rewarding consequences.

How was this radically new way of life accomplished? We now know that it is possible to put living organisms on a schedule of delayed reward purely through *positive* reinforcement, with no punishment whatever. Scientists at the Institute for Behavioral Research in Silver Spring, Maryland, have done so with monkeys, gradually lengthening the interval between action and reward until the monkeys "work" a full eight-hour day to receive their "pay" of food pellets only after twenty-four-hour intervals. But it is not likely that Neolithic man was weaned over to delayed reward without a great deal of aversive control. The various religious sanctions that serve as behavioral codes seem to have become considerably more complex and powerful during this period of prehistory. The whole idea of punishment as a prime education tool was probably born with the Agricultural Revolution.

It is certain that by the time the ancient cities of Mesopotamia and Egypt sprang up along the Fertile Crescent, both specialization and long-delayed reward were rampant. Lewis Mumford has advanced the idea that the kings of those cities, invoking sanctions of divinity, created precisely the highly structured, rigid, ordered "utopias" that Plato and later utopianists were to write about. In so doing, Mumford theorizes, the kings made pawns of people and, indeed, created of them the first great machine: "a machine that concentrated energy in great assemblages of men, each unit shaped, graded, trained, regimented, articulated, to perform its particular function in a unified working whole. . . . The division of tasks and the specialization of labor to which Adam Smith imputes so much of the success of the so-called industrial revolution actually were already in evidence in the Pyramid Age, with a graded bureaucracy to supervise the whole process." This power system, Mumford observes, "was kept in operation by threats and penalties, rather than by rewards. Not for nothing was the king's authority represented by a scepter, for this was only a polite substitute for the mace, that fearful weapon by which the king would kill, with a single blow on the head, anyone who opposed his will."

Indeed, the most common teaching machine of the age

of agriculture was the mace or its less absolute counterpart, the whip. And its teaching may be summed up in the demand, often enforced on penalty of death, that each human individual develop only a fragment of his potential abilities. That man could respond even to this negative education constitutes high tribute to his adaptability as a learner. But the unfortunate side effects of education by punishments—including avoidance reaction, increased tendency toward aggression, hypertension, ulcers, tics, hysteria and all the various and subtle array of neuroses and psychoses—have now been convincingly demonstrated. These side effects were only part of the price men paid for the first great civilized cities. Some of the other costs, as listed by Lewis Mumford, were "total submission to a central authority, forced labor, lifetime specialization, inflexible regimentation, one-way communication and readiness for war."

The price is still being paid. The conditions listed above have a familiar ring, for they have been only ameliorated and rationalized, not basically changed, during the years since early Egypt.

The invention of "reason," for example, was an ingenious way of internalizing the whip, for the concept itself comes into being only as separate from and opposed to feelings, emotions, impulse. Too often, indeed, such terms as "conscience," "dignity," "stoicism," "heroism," "honor" or even "glory" have constituted ultimately indefinable variations on a single theme: man's endeavor to act and speak in a manner aversive to him *without* the prod of external punishment. During the entire period of Civilization, a large measure, perhaps a majority, of an individual's education was devoted to teaching him how to be less than he could be and to perform this feat with the aid of no external taskmaster whatever. The whip securely tucked inside, Lord Raglan's rider could charge the cannons at Balaclava with a narrow smile and a quip. And Central High's honor student can sit day after day, mute and almost uncomplaining, as his perceptions, his world, himself are sliced into little pieces.

Internalizing the whip made possible societies with more agreeable facades than those of the ancient cities. At the same time, the very conditions cited by Mumford—central authority, forced labor, lifetime specialization, inflexible regimentation, one-way communication and readiness for war—could be far more highly developed than would have been possible before the invention of reason, conscience, honor and the like. With a stiff upper lip, the "free" citizens of Imperial Britain under Victoria proudly suffered conditions of life that would have required hordes of taskmasters in ancient Mesopotamia. The U.S. Civil Service employee, sitting atop a giant pyramid of regulations, can find *reasons* for doing almost anything he really does not want to do.

In all of this, the final reinforcer has been negative. Behind each "progressive" teacher (if you will look there in the shadows) stand the stern vice-principal, the truant officer, the policeman. At the heart of every academic honor code dwell expulsion, disgrace.

Since its beginning in the Agricultural Revolution, the period we shall be calling "Civilization" has marched relentlessly, if not steadily, toward ever more subtle and ingenious means of internalized, negative control, toward the goal of "voluntary" individual submission to group functioning. Throughout Civilization, individuals have learned to do their duty: to provide human components for a larger working whole, thus renouncing individual wholeness. "Distrust impulse. Deny feeling." The whip inside—wielded by codes, ethics, *words*—flogs incessantly.

In the verbal arts, Civilized Man has cried his plight to the heavens. The most memorable word practitioners—Ecclesiastes, Sophocles, Dostoevsky, Freud—have chanted the same great tragedy of fragmentation and waste of human potential. Freud, standing at the extreme, the very climax of Civilization itself (Victorian, upper-middle-class Jewish, middle European), composed perhaps the most sorrowful metaphor of all, finding man limited, lashed, broken, condemned to eternal war with himself. He made two main mistakes: thinking himself a scientist rather than a man of letters and believing he was writing about ultimate nature of Man rather than the immediate plight of Civilized Man *in extremis*.

Someday (a thousand, a hundred years from now, or perhaps even tomorrow) men may look back at all these last 150 centuries as a darkly tragic if necessary transition period. The future may weep at what humans endured and wonder that they did indeed endure, that they found it possible to sacrifice themselves to build the man-made environment which, linking all the globe in response and interaction, could at last bring to an end the long Dark Age called "Civilization."

During the period of Civilization, *societies* learned. The conditions under which they learned imposed a moratorium on the full development of *individual* learning. Though there have always been exceptions (as we shall see in the next chapter), the vast preponderance of people have been required to learn, in addition to the necessary tricks of their trade, only the body of knowledge and the way of knowing of their particular society, *and no more*. Our present-day IQ tests are as good an example of the cognitive barbed wire that surrounds us as you could hope to find. It is interesting to note that it takes only sixteen years to master the ground rules that operate within our society's well-guarded compound. After sixteen, it turns out, there is rarely any further "growth" in "intelligence," "reasoning ability" or what have you. And how could there be, with our every "educational" facility bent on the civilizing process? By six, the child is measurably slowed as a free-ranging learner; by sixteen, he is through. The prison gates are locked, the key thrown away. Within the compound, some are better at playing the game than others and are rewarded accordingly.

For those who would break through the barbed wire, each society has devised a multitude of little deaths—loss of status, polite contempt, ostracism, the analyst's couch, the mental ward. Nor has physical death itself seemed too hard a deterrent against real individual learning during the Civilized Epoch; many of the great martyrs barely tested the boundaries of their time.

With human beings as well-regulated components, societies went about their business of learning, changing the conditions of life on this planet. They learned to organize larger and larger social entities, widening the circle inscribed by a campfire's gleam to cover half the globe. This particular learning must have been richly reinforced, for each society has had a powerful tendency to go on aggrandizing far beyond the point where the rewards stopped. The extinction curve of empire is long, cruel and destructive. Destroyed, empire begins again. And through all this gathering up, sweeping together, bringing into bondage, societies have gone on building toward the total, man-made environment that would finally end Civilization itself. They built laboriously, in fits and starts, at incalculable human cost. They built the Sphinx at Giza, the Acropolis, China's Great Wall. They built armies and navies and colonial administrative systems. They built roads and vehicles to move upon them and conduits for

water and markets and modes of exchange. They built
London:

> I wander thro' each charter'd street,
> Near where the charter'd Thames does flow,
> And mark in every face I meet
> Marks of weakness, marks of woe.
>
> In every cry of every Man,
> In every Infant's cry of fear,
> In every voice, in every ban,
> The mind-forg'd manacles I hear.

From his sanctuary of poetical mysticism, William Blake
could hear "the mind-forg'd manacles." Civilization might
need to call Blake mad, or—since he had sanctuary—eccen-
tric. But there have been many other clear-seeing mystics
and visionaries, even in the "highest" (most structured and
technological) of all civilizations, the Greek-Roman-West-
ern. On the other hand, almost every utopian writer in
this lineage—from Plato through More, Bacon, Andreae,
Campanella up to the modern anti-utopianists—has created
a dream worse than reality. Utopia almost invariably cari-
catures the Civilized condition, being more highly structured, more rigidly ordered, more concerned with an
unchanging, mechanistic technology. Only recently have
we begun to see the truth: that most utopias have constituted blueprints, not of hope, but of despair and surrender.

Throughout Civilization, *order* at whatever cost has
seemed the most reliable bulwark against every threat. But
it has been a particular kind of order—not the elegant, interlocking, responsive, self-regenerating order of a natural
ecological system, but a sort of artificial, disjointed, precarious order, in constant danger of collapse from within
and without, propped up only by massive human energy

applied in safely stereotyped fashion. Little wonder that Man and Nature have so long seemed opposite, irreconcilable.

But now Civilization as it has existed for 15,000 years is ending and a new kind of order, a new kind of education are upon us. The old mode of life does not end gracefully or peacefully. The greatest wars, outrages, catastrophes ever known accompany its death throes. It does not end simultaneously everywhere around the world; while new African nations lust after the accouterments of industrial nationalism, the U.S.A.—at least the leading edge—finds itself drawn beyond those very strictures.

McLuhan has said that the African nations, having missed the industrial revolution, may find it easier to adjust to what he calls the "postliterate, retribalized" condition than will the advanced Western nations. Perhaps. In any case, the global communications network can narrow the perceptual and aspirational gap between nations more rapidly than we might expect.

What has happened, indeed, is simpler than it may seem from our present site on the battleground between past and future. Up until now, building and maintaining man-made environments—farms, cities, pyramids, production lines, colonial empires, H-bombs—has required great, even desperate expenditures of human energy. It has demanded the kind of specialization that limits the education of full human potential. But Civilization, it has been argued, made possible leisure, which then made possible the flowering of the arts, humanities and sciences—the "finer things" of human existence. So it did. It made possible a tiny elite of specialists who could turn certain fragments of themselves to these finer things. Most worked within carefully laid-out boundaries. Almost all were male. The artists among them were allowed to engage in the strangely paradoxical business of creating "beauty" out of the waste and horror of their times. Art, indeed, is Civilization's palliative, a ration of rum for the fo'c'sle hands, a bright hallucinogen within prison walls. Matthew Arnold could write that the world "hath really neither joy, nor love, nor light,/ Nor certitude, nor peace, nor help for pain;/ And we are here as on a darkling plain," and, in the very act of setting down those words, contradict them. For how, we ask, can a world in which such beauty exists really be a darkling plain?

Civilization has not, of course, been able to destroy completely the models of individual learning. Social systems are simply too inefficient. (Some of the best arguments against tyranny have been arguments against efficiency.) But the last two centuries in the West (and more recently throughout most of the rest of the world) have seen an exponential increase in the old efficiency.

The death throes of almost every form of life and learning, whether brachiopod, dinosaur, empire or artistic period, is generally marked by grotesque extremes—giantism, overspecialization, supercomplexity and other thrashings about. Civilization reached its extreme, its death throes during the age of mass production, not so long ago. That was when human beings were treated, literally, as components of the social machine, as replaceable and expendable commodities. That was when specialization and standardization ran amok, creating such close resemblance between individuals within a specialty that narrow competition became just about the only way that people could be distinguished one from the other. Competition became the chief ostensible motive force in Western mass education, as it seemed more and more to imitate the production line, with grades, honors and tests of all kinds gathering about them a power and glory all out of proportion to their quite limited function as learning aids. The departmental structure of U.S. higher education, with its proliferating disciplines breaking down into even more subdisciplines, may be looked upon as a model, if not a parody, of Civilization's final extreme.

All of this is reasonably easy to view. It is slightly more difficult to realize how fast it is all passing away. Civilization, the period that began some 15,000 years ago, is over, though its aftereffects will linger for a long time to come. It ended when the man-made environment began to take on the characteristics of a natural ecology, that is, when it became interlocking, responsive and self-regenerating. All this has happened, if only in its crude beginnings, within the last few decades. The worldwide communications satellite, science writer Arthur C. Clarke believes, will be more powerful than the ICBM in changing the world.

At the same time, production lines are yielding to electronically controlled, computerized devices that can produce any number of varying things out of the same material. Already, most U.S. automobiles are, in a sense, custom-built by highly responsive machines. Figuring all possible combinations of styles, options and colors available on a new Thunderbird, for example, a computer expert came up with twenty-five million different versions of it for a buyer. When automated electronic production is more fully developed, it will be just about as cheap and easy to turn out a million differing objects as a million exact duplicates.

Even more important, computers are now learning to build other computers, to repair or update defective computers, to set up communications systems of their own, to plan marketing operations and handle distribution—i.e., to build and maintain self-regenerating systems. When tens of thousands of these computers all over the world are hooked together with access to the virtually unlimited power supply available with nuclear energy; when all people have gained increasingly sophisticated and responsive access to this worldwide ecology; then the limiting, fragmenting conditions of Civilized life will not only be unnecessary, but impossible.

Space technologist Dr. Simon Ramo has described a merchandising system, already technically feasible, in which a product could be conceived and marketed before a single actual model is built. In this system, a designer (or a computer) could conceive a new consumer product. Computers could then figure the optimal size, colors, price and other details of the product and produce a TV "commercial" in which the product (not yet built, mind you) would be featured. Viewers who wish to order it would push a certain button on their sets. (Other buttons would specify color, style, quantity, etc.) This action would instantaneously transfer money credits from the viewers' bank account to the corporation's account. When enough monetary credit is thus accumulated, computer-controlled machinery could start turning out the actual products and sending them to the consumers.

But such futurism, even if imminent, is not necessary to explain what is happening to "human nature." The U.S. housewife drifting dreamlike along the mazes of a supermarket is example enough. No Civilized Calvinist is she, but rather a Polynesian plucking breadfruit as she wanders. This breadfruit, however, has been brought together for her from all over the world—figs from Greece, beer from Japan, caviar from Russia, wines from France. Such an ample Eden would have been inconceivable to those who perpetuated and embellished even the most glittering myths of the Civilized Epoch.

Nor is there any waiting. Reward is immediate. (Regret

for indulgence may come later.) And with time-payment plans for everything from socks to automobiles to houses (and even for cash), the entire system of delayed reward has been turned topsy-turvy. This is like saying that Civilization itself has been overthrown, for a dominant bulk of the social practices and sanctions since agriculture has been based ultimately upon the need for long-delayed gratification. In 1966, the leading American thrift association was quietly disbanded, but the event might well have been heralded by the trumpets of a new age. The fact is, in the post-Civilized era, thrift in the old sense would prove ruinous. And this situation can be reversed only by turning technology around, a doubtful eventuality.

Specialization and standardization as we now know them also seem doomed by the new man-made ecology as it becomes ever more interactive, responsive and self-regenerative. The chief arguments for this possibility have usually come, direfully, from those straight-line extrapolators who cry out that cybernation will take over so many jobs as to create massive unemployment. These men cannot conceive a society without *jobs*. But *job* is an invention of Civilization, a short word that tells its own long story of entrapment, enclosure and fragmentation. Of course, there will be no jobs as we now think of them. Already, electronic devices run elevators, draw blueprints, analyze X rays and perform a myriad of other specialized and standardized jobs. Let the devices have *all* the jobs and let human beings go on with the business they interrupted 15,000 years ago—but now on a far higher, more complex, more joyous level.

Soon the man-made environment will be able to take care of itself, to interact with itself and with human beings just as did the natural ecology in the time of the hunter. Then men will be free again to range the new wilds, to explore possibilities, to probe, to create—in short, to *learn*. The chain of individual learning, broken for this long while, can resume. Challenged by the new environment, the human learner will undoubtedly astound himself. And this will require no further selective breeding, for the brain as is has so much stretch in it as to make eugenics irrelevant during the foreseeable future. From the new situation can come a new kind of order; not a precarious, painful order built by breaking humanity into pieces and trying to fit the pieces together, but the elegant order of a fully functioning world environment that elicits wholeness and lifelong learning from each individual.

Recently, computers programmed to play chess have been giving chess masters a few scares before going down to defeat against superior human "intelligence." The day may come when the computers start winning. For some of those who have not practiced looking beyond Civilization, this may seem a dark day indeed. But others will cheer. Playing chess is not what being human is all about (though programming a computer for competition may be a diverting game). It is oddly but characteristically pessimistic to think that ratiocinating machines will "take over." Ratiocination itself may someday be looked upon as another form of drudgery. The day a computer becomes World Champion of Chess could well be (if we have prepared wisely for the future) merely another step toward ultimate human freedom.

"You can't know what it's like to be alive until you've been a thief in a dark room where someone is sleeping. There's no way I can tell you—how *awake* you are, how much you can hear—you can hear with your skin—how much you *know*. There's a police car moving over there three blocks away. You *know* it's there. You sense it. You *feel* it moving. . . ."

5. THE ROGUE AS TEACHER

My friend is a successful novelist, a journalist, a critic. As a teen-ager, however, he had been a member of a gang of thieves. Now he was telling me what all of us keep forgetting to acknowledge: that the Civilized condition, while nurturing us, robs us of the chance to be all that we could be. Our fascination with every rogue, every free-roving adventurer from Ulysses through Tom Jones, Jesse James, John Dillinger to James Bond reveals an impulse toward lawlessness in us all. Civilization's songs, tales and chronicles are filled with rascals. Maybe it is more than entertainment.

Take fairy tales and children's stories. There is a moment in Kenneth Grahame's *The Wind in the Willows* (written in the early 1900s) when the irrepressible Mr. Toad finds himself in the presence of the one thing most forbidden to him, a motorcar.

> "I wonder," he said to himself presently, "I wonder if this sort of car *starts* easily?"
>
> Next moment, hardly knowing how it came about, he found he had hold of the handle and was turning it. As the familiar sound broke forth, the old passion seized on Toad and completely mastered him, body and soul. As if in a dream he found himself, somehow, seated in the driver's seat; as if in a dream, he pulled the lever and swung the car round the yard and out through the archway; and, as if in a dream, all sense of right and wrong, all fear of obvious consequences, seemed temporarily suspended. He increased his pace, and as the car devoured the street and leapt forth on the high road through the open country, he was only conscious that he was Toad once more, Toad at his best and highest, Toad the terror, the traffic-queller, the Lord of the lone trail, before whom all must give way or be smitten into nothingness and everlasting night. He chanted as he flew, and the car responded with sonorous drone; the miles were eaten up

under him as he sped he knew not whither, fulfilling his instincts, living his hour, reckless of what might come to him.

For his action, Mr. Toad suffers the full weight of the law. He is tried, convicted, sentenced, loaded with chains and dragged "shrieking, praying, protesting" to "the remotest dungeon of the best-guarded keep of the stoutest castle in all the length and breadth of Merry England."

Toad's high moment, and his punishment as well, speak to us from Civilization's forbidden lectern, as does Milton's Satan, gloriously unrepentant, the penultimate crosser of boundaries, doomsday enemy of The System:

> . . . Farewell happy fields
> Where joy forever dwells: Hail horrors, hail
> Infernal world, and thou profoundest Hell
> Receive thy new possessor: one who brings
> A mind not to be changed by place or time.
> The mind is its own place, and in itself
> Can make a Heav'n of Hell, a Hell of Heav'n.
> What matter where, if I be still the same,
> And what I should be, all but less than he
> Whom thunder hath made greater? Here at least
> We shall be free. . . .

It is not all Milton's doing that his Satan makes our blood run fast, or that his God is a pompous, flat, insufferable bore. We should not wonder that the man in the black hat often engages our support, that the lost cause seems the best cause, that bystanders cheered Britain's Great Train Robbers as they came to court, that a vision of Persian orgy dwells in every Shriner's heart. Do not assume that all of this reflects some incurable perversity in mankind or that it tells us anything about the "nature" of man, but instead that it may inform us on the subject of education. For I should like to propose that it is precisely those people who, for whatever reason, have operated *outside* Civilization's strictures who have carried the torch of learning to us across the centuries.

These people are varied. They are the rogue. The common criminal is not among them. Most criminals, after their initial break with pattern, fall into repetitive, stereotyped behavior that apes society itself. Criminologists look for the "MO" (*modus operandi*) by which the criminal gives himself away. The true rogue has no obvious MO. Whether fictional or historical, he is the man of many devices, constantly exploring, probing the environment— learning.

That this master learner to whom we give our secret admiration is so frequently associated with crime and violence may simply indicate that, under the conditions of our Civilization, it is often difficult to go on learning for very long without breaking the law. "There's no crime on Bimini," a visiting reporter remarked, "because nothing's illegal." Bimini may not be an oasis of learning, but neither is Merry England. The point is not that the future-trending educator should encourage violence or disruption, but that he *recognize* the many new means, now clear on the horizon, for making lifelong learning legal, for making it possible, in the poet Herrick's words, for men to be "nobly wild, not mad."

Rogues come in numerous varieties. For our purposes, we may take four, blending fact and fiction, as our tutors: (1) the ordinary rogue or rascal, the adventurer, the *picaro;* (2) the radical technologist; (3) the mystic; (4) the artist.

The first of these need detain us only a moment. His tradition is secure, his fascination universal. "The conditions of civilized living do much to sap our lives of adventure and risk," J. Bronowski writes in his book *The Face of Violence*. "We take our revenge by equating spirit with lawlessness and adventure with the criminal." But we seek extraordinary criminals as our teachers: Jean Laffite, the pirate; or, better still, Sir Francis Drake and all those sea captains who pirated under the legitimizing colors of patriotism; Robin Hood, who somehow has come to represent a one-man United Fund Drive; Black Bart, who posted doggerel verse on the stagecoaches he robbed.

War, conquest and politics may be viewed as means of sanctioning roguery. In these endeavors, men are sometimes freed to burst through the restraining barriers of Civilized living and become free-roving hunters again, going "beyond themselves," performing feats of endurance, skill and clairvoyance they had no reason to anticipate. Stable societies have simply been unable, thus far, to provide the opportunities, the reinforcing contingencies that would make possible going beyond ourselves in the happier and far less limiting fields of brotherhood, love, communion, discovery.

What has perhaps not been noted is that rogues throughout history generally have been closely linked with the latest technology of their times. Just as Ulysses was a master mariner in the early age of seafaring, the highwaymen, cony catchers and vagrants of Europe were men of the open road at a time when the confining dominance of household and guild were waning. And the master rogue of our day, James Bond (with all his imitators), is nothing if not technological. Indeed, the new global spy is purely an instrument of technology. He violates the old boundaries of time, place, conscience and probability. He strikes directly at our old, secure faith in the impossible. His mission is distant and detached from the personal lives of the main actors in the drama. His boss is not the stern, hated, feared, loved "Old Man" of earlier conflicts but, like himself, a cool technician. Sex is an icy pleasure that is best when taken by force or deception from an enemy.

And, above all, technology is supreme. In the Bond movies, our laughter at the mechanical, electronic and chemical outrages is a laughter of recognition, not ridicule. Bond is the foremost free-roving hunter in the new global jungle of interlocking technology. By his double-O code designation, he is identified as one licensed to kill. Thus law sanctions the outlaw. But what this rogue may be teaching us—in the absurd triumph of impersonality (and possibly its end)—is that the final victim is actually society as we know it, Civilization itself.

The radical technologist, second among our rogues, figures in some of Civilization's most persistent myths. These myths—cautionary tales on a grand scale—show the bringer of or seeker after new technologies succeeding for a while, then suffering his dire desserts. Prometheus is the archetype, and fire may be said to represent all the new technologies. The fire-bringer's suffering serves warning on all who would tamper with the basic technological framework of any society and emphasizes an essential truth: *Any radical change in the technology within an established order will surely bring that order down.*

Indeed, those who would conserve and perpetuate any social entity are quite correct in fearing new knowledge and opposing all innovators who step across the lines that circumscribe Civilized man's every move. Establishment warnings against new technology come down to us across the ages. "Blest pair," wrote Milton of Adam and Eve; "and O yet happiest if ye seek/ No happier state, and know to know no more." Daedalus warned Icarus to fly neither too high nor too low. The Tower of Babel, according to archeological deductions, was simply a temple in the form of a ziggurat and was not meant by the Babylonians to threaten God but to worship him. But to the Israelites (who wrote the story) the tower was a threat. The Babylonians stood at a high stage of technology for their time and were building in an impressive manner. Such a technology might have destroyed Hebraic society; better not understand it.

During the medieval period, fear of all novelty reached a high state and was reflected even in the language. The Arabic word *bid'a* means "novelty," but it also means "heresy." The Spanish word *novedad* carries similar undertones.

The Renaissance view of just who the devil was came clear in the legend of Faust: the devil, it turned out, was none other than the master technologist himself, the very same one who had led Adam and Eve out of their happy ignorance. To follow his forbidden knowledge as Faust did was to lose one's soul. This warning came at a time when new technology was shattering all the usual forms of existence throughout Europe. In the legend, the threatening technology was presented as old-fashioned medieval magic. Nothing surprising about this; as McLuhan has repeatedly pointed out, the content of each new environment is invariably the old environment itself; man drives into the future with his eyes fixed firmly on the rearview mirror.

Christopher Marlowe in 1588 presented the Faust story in dramatic form, and his *Doctor Faustus* became immensely popular. Traveling troupes brought it even to small villages all across Europe. In several versions, including puppet plays, the traditional Faust story retained its popularity well into the nineteenth century, long after Goethe's literary treatment.

The question here is whether people flocked to see the

Faust plays to be warned about the dangers of following devilish knowledge or simply out of fascination with a marvelous rogue. For Faust steps restlessly across Civilization's most rigid barriers, inspired, it seems, by nothing more than a spirit of curiosity. "Possessed of omnipotent magic," Richard G. Moulton has written, "Faustus does not use his power for profound speculations, or schemes of self-aggrandizement; he flits like a bee from flower to flower of casual suggestion; he is ready to go to hell for the sake of a new sensation." He is, in short, a learner.

A nineteen-year-old girl named Mary Wollstonecraft wrote the archetypal modern tale of the rogue-technologist just after being married to the poet Shelley. She called her work *Frankenstein, or The Modern Prometheus. Frankenstein* was published in London in 1818 and quickly became a best seller. The first dramatic version was staged in London in 1823. A handbill advertising the play read: "The striking moral exhibited in this story is the fatal consequence of that presumption which attempts to penetrate, beyond prescribed depths, into the mysteries of nature." Frankenstein, the creator, is still with us, suffering, time and again, the fatal consequence of his presumption. Invariably, he is unhappy beyond human endurance and generally shares violent death with the monster he has created. Various stage adaptations have had the monster being caught in an avalanche, hit by a thunderbolt, falling into Mount Aetna, drowned in an Arctic storm and leaping from a high crag. The cinema has added death in a burning mill, in an explosion and in a cauldron of boiling sulfur. *Sic semper technologists.*

What concerns us here is not the literary quality of Frankenstein and the endless progeny of mad scientists who peer at us through their thick glasses from behind all that intricate tubing in comic books and horror movies, but the universal bewitchery they hold for us. These rogues have something powerful to teach: radical change in technology will change human life in a way Marx could not have dreamed. This process of change itself moves from what is known to what is unknown. Fearing that, we fear the technologist. And with reason: the H-bomb is the ultimate Faustian tool.

But joyful and intelligent engagement, not paralyzing fear or stubborn resistance, may be the appropriate response. The monster may well be amenable—not just the bomb, which can serve as an oversimplification, but the whole pervasive network of new technology. In the early 1800s, the Luddites roamed the English countryside, destroying the textile machinery they feared would create an economic disaster. But the disaster did not occur; the riots ended. Recently, a history professor at the University of California informed me that technology would *not* change the human condition because, in his words, "there are enough people like me who will go out and smash the computers before that can happen."

Professors *vs.* computers? It could happen, though the professors will probably find their worst fears, like the Luddites', are groundless. It is useless to pretend, however, that the established order will survive unaltered. Revolution by technology is far more effective than by ideology or violence. In violent political revolutions, only the hangmen change; the gallows remain the same. Technological revolution, on the other hand, razes the entire structure. The cautionary tales are generally in vain, since technology has a way of creeping in unseen. When the revolution at last becomes visible, the guardians of things-as-they-are may react with confusion and panic. These guardians include entrenched politicians, traditionalists of all stripes and a surprisingly large segment of the academic and intellectual community. The latter is known to be liberal, openminded and innovative, but not beyond prescribed depths. Much academic and intellectual energy, in fact, goes toward building and mending the perceptual fences within which established specialists feel their disciplines must operate. It is precisely these fences the rogue-technologist would leap.

A third rogue, the mystic, can be the most dangerous of all, since he is a technologist of the inner being. His works do not always upset traditions. Revelation has been buttressed with hierarchy as rigid as any known to Civilization. Mystical practices have helped, as in India, to perpetuate structured societies. *But beware*. At any moment, the mystical impulse can bring the structure down. For mysticism admits no boundaries whatever, not even the minimal interface between self and other. Logic, knowledge, proportion all may fall. The Upanishads hold that Enlightenment lies *beyond* the Golden Orb, that is, the very best of conventional wisdom.

For us of the West, there is no better example of the mystic as rogue than Jesus. He followed his vision all the way, though the changes he preached would have unglued the entire reinforcement structure of Civilization, replacing law with love. He formulated perhaps the most revolutionary educational prescription ever known: "Except ye be converted, and become as little children, ye shall not enter into the kingdom of heaven." Any respectable citizen would have to be far removed, in time and place, from Calvary to think Jesus anything other than a rogue. It may be an indictment of our time that we no longer consider Him so.

The artist, last of the rogues considered here, teaches us more explicitly than the rest. Unlike the rascal, the radical technologist and the mystic, he often has enjoyed his own society's sanction for his roguery. Like Agent 007, he is licensed to kill. Make no mistake about it, the great artist must destroy the forms and perceptions of his time. He must seek order that confounds order. He must journey beyond the conscience of his race.

The more highly specialized and repressed a society becomes, the more it needs Art as a separate category, a place that is safe for wholeness, for feelings, for learning. Primitive man did not see Art apart from life. He seems to have been indifferent toward his cave paintings or sculpture once it was completed; we find the same cave wall painted over again and again. The important thing was not the finished work itself, but the act of making it. Even as late as the Renaissance, artists could be thought of in somewhat the same terms as craftsmen. And Bach revealed his views on the permanence of his work by sometimes using manuscripts to wrap his lunch.

As fragmentation and categorization continued apace, however, the artist found himself pushed off to one side into his own special niche, where he often was granted a tentative amnesty for his "eccentricities." The most repressed and rigid societies (say Victorian England), societies that permitted their male members no outward display of emotion, allowed their artists to exhibit Bohemian ways, to be effusive or melancholy or even tearful. And then these societies *used* the completed works of art as safety valves for their own bottled-up feelings. They tried to imprison them in heavy, stolid buildings they called "art museums," or in other museums they called "symphony halls" and "opera houses." But the artist is a rogue and eventually can be neither imprisoned nor classified. Always a jump ahead of the technologist, the artist in recent times has been attempting to cross all of Civilization's boundaries. Today, in the Happenings and total-environ-

ment events of the young, we may watch the ultimate barrier—that between artist and audience—being torn down,
brick by brick. It may turn out that the contemporary
artist is engaged in the business of ending Art, thereby
helping us create an environment in which each individual
life may be lived as a work of art.

In the meantime, the rogue-artist provides us one of the
best learning programs to be found in the whole crumbling
schoolhouse of Civilization. He demonstrates the interplay
between discipline and freedom, contending with the limitations of his materials, yet never failing to find (if he is a
true artist) that the materials are less limiting than was
previously thought. He reveals for us, in his way of working, what the Indian mystic Sri Aurobindo called the soul's
distrust of all absolutes. He is compelled toward the particular, the place, the moment. "Art does not generalize
and classify," writes Suzanne Langer; "art sets forth the
individuality of forms which discourse, being essentially
general, has to suppress. The sense of life is always new,
infinitely complex, therefore infinitely variable in its possible expressions."

The artist revives in us the senses and feelings and aspects of being that Western Civilization, in its pell-mell
pursuit of the purely verbal-symbolic-conceptual, has
caused many of us quite to neglect in the educational endeavor. He shows us how to explore the sensory universe.
He maps for us the many roads to delight.

To play, to dally, to caper—these are the true modes of
creation. History shouts the lesson; we refuse to hear. We
forget that, in Eric Hoffer's words,

> man's most unflagging and spectacular efforts were made
> not in search of necessities but of superfluities. . . . The
> utilitarian device, even when it is an essential ingredient
> of our daily life, is most likely to have its ancestry in the

nonutilitarian. The sepulchre, temple and palace preceded the utilitarian house; ornament preceded clothing; work, particularly teamwork, derives from play. We are told that the bow was a musical instrument before it became a weapon, and some authorities believe that the subtle craft of fishing originated in a period when game was abundant—that it was the product not so much of grim necessity as of curiosity, speculation, and playfulness. We know that poetry preceded prose, and it may be that singing came before talking. . . . On the whole it seems to be true that the creative periods in history were buoyant and even frivolous. . . . One suspects that much of the praise of seriousness comes from people who have a vital need for a facade of weight and dignity. La Rochefoucauld said of solemnity that it is "a mystery of the body invented to conceal the defects of the mind."

The artist, like all rogues, mocks solemnity. And he shows us how to be nobly wild, not mad. Psychologist Frank Barron of the University of California and his colleagues have conducted intensive studies of highly creative people who have achieved recognition in their fields—writing, painting, sculpturing, music, architecture. It is particularly interesting to note that, on the most widely used personality test (the Minnesota Multiphasic Personality Inventory), the successful creators rank up with institutionalized schizophrenics on the Schizophrenia Scale. However, on an Ego Strength Scale, the creative people rate high, the schizophrenics, low.

We may interpret these findings as testifying to the usefulness of controlled madness. The unusual perceptions, heightened sensory vigilance and unexpected visions of the madman perhaps exist to some extent in every genius who would move the boundaries of his time. The "successful" creators differ from the institutionalized unfortunates in that they can give their visions form—and also in that they have learned the disguises and dissimulations required by the world-as-it-is. Some of the remaining shamanistic societies (the Bantu of south Africa, the Tanala of Madagascar and the Mojave of the southwest U.S., for example) have found ways to reap social worth from extreme "schizophrenia." And indeed, a growing number of present-day psychologists and psychiatrists are beginning to feel that it is quite possible for us to create a world safer for man's errant impulses, a world that would yield us more color, richness and ecstasy *without* repressions, violence and war.

The rogue, nobly wild, teaches us the first elementary lesson about a life in which one does not have to break law or custom in order to come fully awake; a life in which new technology—whether outside or inside the human organism—is not feared and resisted, but deflected toward humane uses; a life in which every established order takes as its first task the business of making itself obsolete; a life in which society's main function is to evolve into everevolving new societies.

Such a lesson may seem radical. But it may turn out to be a simple drill in current events. The shackles of the past are loosening. And the world is crowded, as always, with rogues. Actually, there are now hundreds of millions of them. They are rascals, radical technologists, mystics and artists. They are original, openminded, clear of vision, adaptable, sensitive, enthusiastic, joyful and graceful. They are anything but fragmented, and their chief pleasure in life is learning. It is with what happens to those rogues, our children, in the years to come that the following chapters are concerned.

THE MOST OBVIOUS BARRIER between our children and the kind of education that can free their enormous potential seems to be the educational system itself: a vast, suffocating web of people, practices and presumptions, kindly in intent, ponderous in response. Now, when true educational alternatives are at last becoming clear, we may overlook the simplest: no school.

6. NO SCHOOL?

This means just what it says: the elimination of educational institutions housed in separate buildings with classrooms and teachers. At the least, it involves the end of all compulsory school attendance. The idea may seem entirely impractical. But the recent development of a technology of individualized learning has changed things. "No school" has now become feasible. Before going on to other alternatives, we might well give this one a fair hearing. The case may be stated as follows: Practically everything that is *presently* being accomplished in the schools can be accomplished more effectively and with less pain in the average child's home and neighborhood playground.

The man who first brought this proposal to my attention is Dr. M. W. Sullivan, the educational programmer whose work was covered briefly in the chapter on the human potential. Sullivan is an outspoken and passionate man, and he argues with the prejudice of one who has seen the power of well-designed self-instructional materials. But I doubt if there is anyone who can state the case better.

Sullivan first began mulling over the "no school" idea in the late 1950s, when he and others at Hollins College in Virginia were developing some of the earliest programmed instruction. Why ship the bodies of our children through crowded streets to overstuffed schools, he wondered, when we can much more easily ship instructional materials to their homes?

> In the entire psychological literature [Sullivan says], you can find no evidence that the teacher *per se* helps learning. You can find much evidence that the teacher does harm to the learning process. The average school, in fact, is no fit place to learn in. It is basically a lock-up, a jail. Its most basic conditions create a build-up of resistance to learning. Physically, the child is worn down by the fatigue of sitting in one position for inordinate lengths of time.

Mentally, he is stunned by the sameness of his surroundings and the monotony of the stimuli that bombard him. Can you imagine the amount of energy it takes just to sit still, waiting, against every impulse, for your turn to respond?

When *you* think, you want to get up, move, pace around. But most schoolrooms are set up to *prevent* thinking, learning, creativity—whatever you want to call it. You'd be surprised how many new teachers are told, "Classroom control must come first. The most important thing the child has to learn is how to take instructions, so if you spend the first two months, or two years, teaching them to take instructions, it will be well worth while."

The average kid gets few chances to respond during the school day. And when he does get a chance, it's generally an echoic response. He just gives the teacher back what the teacher wants to hear. And you end up with an organism that has no integrity at all. Too often, when the organism does break through and start responding, he gets slapped down. He learns to sit still, to line up in orderly rows, to take instructions, to feel guilt for his natural impulses—and perhaps to do a few simple things that he could learn to do one-fiftieth—yes, *one-fiftieth*—of the time it usually takes him.

Now what would happen if you shipped the learning materials to the child rather than shipping the child to the dungeon? Let's assume no technological advances—no computers or electronic consoles. All you'd have to have would be the present form of programmed textbooks plus tapes that could be played on $24.95 Japanese tape recorders equipped with foot pedals. We already have programs for teaching languages and other auditory subject matter; the child goes through a written program, turning on the recorder with a foot pedal wherever stars appear in the program. Thus we can combine all the needed written, visual, auditory stimuli. We can provide any learning of importance that goes on in most present classrooms.

So I would have to say that, even with the present rather primitive programs, even the worst ghetto home can be a better learning environment than most schools. At least in the ghetto home, the child can get up and run around when he wants to. If he can just be kept out of school, he won't be taught that learning is dull, unpleasant work. He'll just assume it's what it is: the greatest pleasure in human life. There'll be no guilt and fear. He'll play with his learning materials when he feels like it. And if it's only a half hour a day, he'll be *far* ahead of school learning in all the basic subjects.

But what of social contacts, I asked Sullivan? What of "learning to get along with others in the peer group?" Sullivan replied:

Is there any indication that such a thing takes place in school? What is this *getting along* or *making out* with others? Why can't children learn that much better in neighborhood playgrounds or on the sidewalks or even in the streets? These bowling-alley places where you leave kids. They're good. Much better than schools where children are subjected to a totally false discipline and totally artificial relationships with each other.

In my own case, I was the only kid in my neighborhood who was sent to kindergarten. It was optional then in Connecticut. So for almost a year my peer group was out playing, learning, creating their own very exciting world while I was being tortured in school. They built a tree-house. They built a hut. And what did I do? I learned how to lie on a mat, how to listen to stories, how to line up, how to sit still. Finally, I figured how to escape. I wet my pants and they sent me home. *They sent me home.* The first time was an accident, but after that I made sure to do it every day. And I was free to learn again.

School is a terrible thing to do to kids. It's cruel, unnatural, unnecessary.

Many people would argue, I reminded Sullivan, that the school is a model of the world. Eventually, the child probably will have to face unpleasant working situations, narrow competition. There will be unreasonable deadlines, hasty instructions that will have to be understood and heeded—all sorts of hardships.

> Yes, I know. The old idea was, if you want the kid to get along in life, you put him in that situation as soon as possible. If he's going to be in a lousy situation where he feels inadequate later, you put him in a lousy situation where he feels inadequate now. It just doesn't work that way. There was a very interesting study made on those Marines in World War II who went through the worst campaigns of the war, the ones who hit Guadalcanal and went through the whole thing—boredom, jungle rot, water up to the waist in foxholes, people dying all around them. As it turned out, the guy who stands up under all this is the one who would be considered to have had a very fortunate childhood, the good boy who was always told he was good. And who cracks wide open? The person who had been up against tough conditions in his childhood, with all sorts of hardships, the guy who had never had a chance at success.
>
> You see, the whole argument falls apart however you look at it, even in the extreme case of the Marines in combat. But the world is generally not that extreme. The world isn't any damned way. It's what people make it. You can go a long way toward making your world. And that's just where the school steps in. It warps your expectations so that you'll see the outside world like the school and then you'll tend to make your world that way. You'll be trained to see learning as hard and painful. And you'll go out and perpetuate a world in which those conditions exist.
>
> You know, you have to *teach* any organism how to be

unhappy. And the human being is the only organism that has *learned* unhappiness—except maybe some of his has spilled over onto his dog. I must insist that schools as they now exist are well-designed to produce unhappiness and little else.

At this point, I felt constrained to raise the most powerful objection of all. "Whatever you say," I told Sullivan, "the mothers won't buy it. They just don't want their kids around the house, under their feet all day."

You're probably right. It's strange. They're so anxious to have the kids, then they seem to want to get them out of sight as quickly as possible. We'd have to teach the mothers a different attitude toward their children, not so much goddess and slave as playmates. We'd have to relieve their nervousness about the whole area of book learning. We'd have to show them how to reinforce their children's exploratory behavior whenever possible. Most of all, we'd have to teach them to spend a lot more time just leaving them alone—and perhaps enjoying them.

The trouble is that the parents have been to school, too. If we could just get the kids *out* of school for one generation, we'd solve the whole problem.

Parents who would reject Sullivan's views as extreme have a simple way of checking them out. Arrange for a visit to your child's school—but not on the usual parents' visiting day. (Go then, too, if you wish, but don't expect to find out what really goes on; the teacher and class have probably spent several days or weeks preparing for this charade.) Arrive early in the morning, with your child. Chat for a few moments with the teacher to put him at ease, and allow him to introduce you to the class. Assure him that you plan to create no disturbance whatever but simply to melt into the woodwork. Then take a chair near the back of the room at a position where you have an oblique view of your child. Be natural, casual, friendly. When children turn to look at you, smile slightly in acknowledgment and reassurance, then turn away. If you are natural and at ease, you will probably be surprised at how quickly you are ignored. And, though the teacher may tend to be on guard, his basic style of teaching and relating with the children is generally too deeply ingrained to allow for very much dissembling. You will have the opportunity of experiencing what your child experiences.

Take the opportunity. Focus in on your child. Try to assume his viewpoint, feel what he feels, learn what he learns. Become sensitive to his body positions; see when he sits straight, when he hunches over, when he squirms, when he languishes. Balance the weight of the teacher's words against the pressure on your seat. Try not to daydream. Remember that time goes more slowly for a child than for an adult.

Now are you ready for a little walk? A cup of coffee? A visit to the restroom? A cigarette? Forget it. Stay with your child. Stand only when he stands. Leave the room only when he leaves the room. Concentrate on him. *Become* your child.

Bored beyond endurance? Let us hope not. Let us pray for our children and for all children that you have found one of those master magicians who, in spite of every obstacle, manages to pull each unlikely new moment out of a hat, wiggling and full of life. If not, be easy on yourself for a little while; steal a few moments from the day (though your child has no such opportunity) for a modest experiment. Take out a watch with a second hand. Mark the lines of a sheet of notebook paper with tiny crosshatches, each representing ten seconds. An hour's worth will fit neatly on a single sheet of notebook paper. Select a typical period, say, arithmetic instruction. During this period, mark each ten-second interval during which your child is really *learning* something. Leave the other intervals blank. For a working definition of what learning is, refer to Chapter I. Bear in mind that true learning is change (not needless repetition of something already known) and that the learning has to do with the response of the child, not with the presentation of the teacher.

This little exercise will take sensitivity; you will have to be, in a sense, inside your child's mind. It will be more easily accomplished in the lower grades than in high school (or college, for that matter), where the lecture system makes it virtually impossible to know if learning is taking place. It will involve some guessing and can under no circumstances be termed "scientific." Nonetheless, it will most likely prove a revelation to you. I have tried it with my own children and with scores of others in all sorts of schools. The results are discouraging. Even marking with a kind of desperate generosity, I have rarely been able to fill in more than a third of the intervals. Often I have found that "classroom control" plus waiting for other children to recite plus all the other unwieldy manipulations demanded by the usual classroom environment leave less than ten percent of any child's time for anything that can remotely be termed "learning."

When you have had enough of this exercise, *stay where you are*. No coffee, no cigarettes, no moving around to relax your body and stimulate your thoughts.

Playtime. *Freedom*. Not so fast. First (if you are in a typical classroom), the entire class must come to order. That means stillness, silence. Perhaps each row of children will be pitted against the others; the row achieving submissive nonactivity first gets to line up first at the door. After all the children, again, have come to order and after teacher, again, orders the class to walk, not run, down the stairs, the door is opened. The children explode onto the play yard.

Go with them. Sit down somewhere among them so that you can experience the child's world at the child's level. True learning can take place under the conditions of play. But are you observing *play*? Probably not, unfortunately. The children are likely to be merely letting off steam, with shrill yells and frenetic running about. It has been my experience that, wherever the classroom situation is repressive and antithetical to learning, the playground situation, in direct ratio, is hyperactive and equally antithetical to learning. In true play, the child is intent, responsive, unhurried, completely involved. There is a lovely seriousness about it. The child who explodes out of and in reaction to a static, nonlearning environment is hurried, unresponsive, indeed almost spastic. This is not delight; it is desperation. After experiencing the playground situation, ask yourself, "Is this the kind of social interaction for which I'm sending my child to school?"

Back in class again, then to lunch. And then the afternoon. Does the classroom seem stuffy? Watch the eyes of your child and all the others. Are they becoming heavy with incipient sleep? Are the tender half-moons of delicate skin just beneath them becoming puffy and discolored? Look closely. And how about your own eyes? Do you find yourself stifling yawns? Let us hope not. Let us hope the day has been an exhilarating one.

If not, however, don't hasten to blame the teacher. The environment in which he works, the expectations he tries to fulfill, the techniques generally offered him are woefully inadequate to the human potential. The teacher who prevails over such conditions is an artist, a hero of our times.

And yet do not let compassion for the teacher soften the sense of tragedy that you may feel. The world is filled with wrongs—war, disease, famine, racial degradations and all the slaveries man has invented for his own kind. But none is deeper or more poignant than the systematic, innocent destruction of the human spirit that, all too often, is the hidden function of every school. And do not think that your child can escape unscathed. There has been a lot of speculation lately about LSD's permanently altering the brain structure. This is a naïve way of putting it. First, as pointed out in Chapter II, the brain does not have a set "structure." Second, there is very little that is entirely "permanent" about the behavior of the central nervous system. Learned behavior is generally reversible, though reversing a behavior learned early in life takes a great deal more energy at a later stage than was originally needed to establish the behavior. Still, it might well be said that a number of LSD trips do alter the brain, if only because of the changes wrought through the behaviors engaged in during those trips. This being the case, it must be said that the typical first-grade experience probably alters the brain of your child even more than would many LSD trips, doing untold violence to his potential as a lifelong learner.

"Tragedy" is a strong word, but I can think of no other to describe what happens to most children during the early elementary years. Visiting schools around the country, I have shuttled again and again from a kindergarten room to, say, a fourth grade. (If you have the chance, you might try this for yourself.) And I have talked with hundreds of teachers about the seemingly mysterious human discrepancy revealed on that short journey. It is almost as if you are viewing specimens of two different species. Teachers are the first to agree that this is so. Nor did I receive a single letter of dissent when I described the trip in a *Look* magazine story called "What Your Child Can Teach His Teacher," in December of 1966:

Go into a kindergarten room. By and large, the five-year-olds are spontaneous, unique. Tell them to dance, and they move naturally with a sort of unorganized grace. Read them a story, and their eyes give you back its suspense, fear, laughter. We like to say their faces light up (a particularly telling phrase), and when we look into this illumination, we are not ashamed to let our own faces glow in return. All of this, we assume, is a natural condition of the very young.

Walk down the hall to a fourth-grade classroom. Very quickly, you will notice that something has been lost. Not so many eyes are alight. Not so many responses surprise you. Too many bodies and minds seem locked in painful self-awareness. This, too, we carelessly attribute to the natural order. It's just part of growing up.

But is it really? Is it really necessary for the human animal to lose in spontaneity and imagination as it gains in knowledge and technique? Must we shed the brightness of childhood as we put on the armor plating of age?

Perhaps it is no coincidence that the growth rate of intelligence falls off so rapidly just at the point when the child enters school. Older concepts of how the brain works offered physiological explanations for the startling fact that most humans have achieved eighty percent of their intelligence growth by their eighth birthday. Each new fact, it was said many years ago, makes a little crease or rut in the gray matter. After so long, there is no space for any more ruts. In more recent times, the synapses were said to be somehow "filled up," or the brain cells were "committed." The best recent research, however, as was pointed out in Chapter II, suggests that the brain can never be "filled up." But it can be *taught* to stop learning—that is, changing. It can be *taught* to stop exploring, to reject the unfamiliar, to focus on a limited number of stimuli, to make repetitive, standard responses.

Indeed, the entire education process as it is usually constituted in our schools may best be viewed as a funnel through which every child is squeezed into an ever-narrowing circle; at the end there is room only for a single set of "right answers." The funnel does not stop constricting at the end of the lower grades, or even at high-school graduation. Educator Harold Taylor told me of what he called "four of the most depressing days of my life," with students from each of the four classes of a small, elite Eastern college—one day for each class, starting with freshmen. The experience had the quality of stop-action photography, in which the effects of four years of college were compressed into that many days. The freshmen, Dr. Taylor said, were still, to some extent, open and inquisitive, ready for new ideas. Each subsequent class was less so, with the seniors seeming bored, cynical and interested only in "How will this help me get a better grade?" or "What's in it for me?"

Professor William Arrowsmith goes another step, in writing of his preference for teaching the undergraduate in the humanities rather than the graduate student, whom he finds

> already half-corrupted by the fate he has chosen, the fate which makes him a graduate student. He wants knowledge and information. He has examinations on his mind, and hence tends to conform to his professor's expectation of him—the fate they have jointly chosen and now jointly enforce. The resentment they both frequently feel is their resentment of this mutual fate. For the graduate student, the undergraduate's lucky integration is no longer possible—or if it is, God help him! The present is now less insistent for him. He has chosen to *know* rather than to *be*. For a man with a gift of life, that loss is like castration; the best leave rather than suffer it. Others grit their teeth and will their way through.

It is not that the "product" of our education system is not "capable." He comes out with "skills." He may be a usable component in the social machine. But he is just about finished as a learner.

Only the inefficiency of the present school system and the obdurance of certain individuals can account for the creativity, the learning ability that survives after age twenty-five. Dr. Harold G. McCurdy of the University of North Carolina has studied the childhood patterns of those historical geniuses about whose childhood most is known. Seeking factors common to the early life of the twenty geniuses he selected, Dr. McCurdy came up with three: "(1) a high degree of attention focused upon the child by parents and other adults, expressed in intensive educational measures and, usually, abundant love; (2) isolation from other children, especially outside the family; and (3) a rich efflorescence of phantasy, as a reaction to the two preceding conditions." McCurdy concludes that "the mass education of our public school system is, in its way, a vast experiment on the effect of reducing all three of the above factors to minimal values, and should, accordingly, tend to suppress the occurrence of genius."

When McCurdy refers to public education as an "experiment," he is, unwittingly, taking educators into dangerous territory. For if we *did* consider schooling as experimental in nature, educators might well stand indicted under at least five of the ten essential principles of the Nuremberg Code for research involving human subjects. Imagine your children as the subjects:

1. The voluntary consent of the human subject is absolutely essential.

2. The experiment should be such as to yield fruitful results for the good of society, unprocurable by other

means of study, and not random and unnecessary in nature.

3. The experiment should be designed and based on the results of animal experimentation and a knowledge of the natural history of the disease or other problem under study, so that the anticipated results will justify the performance of the experiment.

4. The experiment should be so constructed as to avoid all unnecessary physical and mental suffering and injury.

5. During the course of the experiment, the human subject should be at liberty to bring the experiment to an end if he has reached the physical or mental state where continuation of the experiment seems to him impossible.

The first and last provisions cited here would seem to be the most grossly violated by the present system of compulsory mass education. That children should be forced by law to stay in school until late adolescence may someday be perceived as outrageous. The current series of public-service advertisements urging adolescents to remain even longer already reveals the crux of the matter:

EDUCATION IS FOR THE BIRDS
The birds that get ahead
or
BOY.
Drop out of school now and that's what
they'll call you all your working life.

Behind the words, society's naked face—patronizing, insulting, ultimately utterly cynical.

But the slogans are true, aren't they? Yes. And there's the trouble. Jobs *are* withheld from those who don't possess a certain diploma. The diplomas, however, are screening devices. The job-dispensing agencies are not really interested in what the job seeker has learned in the school, but merely that, for whatever reason, he has survived it.

When you come right down to it, the amount of learning that goes on in high school, even in the simplest and most explicit techniques of our civilization, is minuscule. Look, for example, at the English textbooks from seventh grade through twelfth. They are basically the same book. And the student who writes and comprehends skillfully in the seventh grade will most likely be doing equally well at high-school graduation and forever after. To quote the recent president of the National Council of Teachers of English, Dr. Alfred H. Grommon: "Forty years of teaching traditional English grammar to American students of varying backgrounds has failed to improve their ability to speak or write it."

Perhaps we should be glad that schools do generally fail in their present task, which is, as I have said before and undoubtedly will say a few more times, to teach a few tricks and otherwise limit possibilities, narrow perceptions and bring the individual's career as a learner (changer) to an end. Such a task may have seemed necessary, if ignoble, in the precarious fragmented society of the past, when individuals, as components, had to prop up the great social machine.

It is the basic premise of this book, however, that the highly interactive, regenerative technological society now emerging will work best, indeed will *require* something akin to mass genius, mass creativity and lifelong learning. If this premise proves out, schools *as they now exist* are already obsolete. And, if someone like Sullivan can provide us with the wherewithal to do at home, easily, painlessly and quickly, what the schools attempt presently to do, in pain and failure, then perhaps we should consider ending the affliction, the tyranny that for so long has entrapped schoolchild and schoolmaster alike—and save billions of dollars in the process. (Linguistic note: The only two entries under the word "disciplinarian" in the index of Roget's *Thesaurus* are "tyrant" and "teacher.")

But let me hasten to stress again that what is usually being taught in school today makes up only a tiny fraction of man's education, present or potential. Nor does programmed instruction offer salvation; it will soon become outmoded. But this mode of learning—and others, such as the new speed-reading technique—provides hope and confidence to those who would expand education's domain and pursue ecstasy in learning. It proves that, *if need be,* we can even now remedy most educational ills that have plagued our children and confounded the "experts" over the years. Excepting the severely handicapped (possibly less than one percent of the population), *every* child can learn to read, to write, to spell, to manipulate quantities, to learn all the hard stuff of present-day schooling—in less than one-third the present time.

We might end schools rather than let them remain as they are today. Except for the legal difficulties, I would prefer having my own children learn at home; I have seen what schools, in spite of every good intention, have subtracted from their lives. But, instead of taking that alternative, we can move on into the unexplored lands of the human potential. We can take that extra two-thirds of present school time available to us right now (as a few experimental schools already are doing) and get on with the most exhilarating experiment in man's history: to help every child become, *in his own way,* an artist; to help every child become, *in his own way,* a genius; to see just how far toward ecstasy and accomplishment every human being can go.

About that day in class, your visit to school: I was not being hypothetical. I seriously recommend that you do it. Most teachers and administrators will probably welcome you. If, however, some administrator should bridle, remind him that you have every educational, moral and legal right to be there. The kind of visit outlined above, one parent a day, creates far less disruption than does a mass visitation on special days or weeks. And anyway (we keep forgetting) the schools belong to us. If they are failing to educate, it is, ultimately, because we don't care enough.

What specific actions will make it possible for us to do it? We do not always answer these questions with words. Or, if we use words, they often have little to do with the real answers. But the answers are there, acknowledged or not, in every administrative directive, every textbook, every teachers' meeting, every classroom. If we are to have schools in the future, how are they to answer the question of human purpose?

Schools and colleges have until now (to recap briefly) served a society that needed reliable, predictable human components. Appropriately enough, they spent overwhelming amounts of time and energy ironing out those human impulses and capabilities that seemed errant. Since learning involves behavioral change, lifelong learning was the most errant of behaviors and was not to be countenanced. Educational institutions, therefore, were geared to *stop* learning. Perhaps half of all learning ability was squelched in the earliest elementary grades, where children found out that there exist predetermined and unyielding "right answers" for everything, that following instructions is what really counts and, most surprisingly, that the whole business of education is mostly dull and painful.

With the bulk of learning ability wiped out in early childhood, the schools could proceed at their own leisure to slow and then still what was left of each human component's capacity to change. The process moved at different rates for different types of components. The simpler ones (unskilled workers, for example) were finished off after only a few years of schooling. Cast to a basic conformation that would last all their lives, they were plugged into the social machine. More complex components took longer to shape. Schooling's most elegant maneuver consisted in braking learning ability so that, for all practical purposes, it would reach zero speed just at the point of graduation.

Exceptions were made. Art, as discussed earlier, could be set aside as a sanctuary for lifelong learning. Another activity, generally termed "the life of the mind," was found to be generally harmless and inconsequential; so it, too, was sanctioned by society even after graduation. Thus the illusion of lifelong learning could be maintained while the organism changed hardly at all beyond its ability to verbalize "concepts."

The process of formal education itself was kept in motion by punishment or the threat of punishment, and by two main positive motivators, narrow competition and eager acquisition. These motivators became answers in themselves to the ultimate questions of life's purpose. Narrow competition, for example, served ends that went far beyond motivation. It produced close resemblance among the individuals involved. (Competition needs specialists who distinguish themselves from one another primarily by doing the *same* thing slightly better or faster.) As much as any other factor, it created the standardization so essential to the highly structured societies of the Civilized Epoch. Individuals who perform unique acts or live unique lives tend to make narrow competition impossible and thereby to throw the traditional social structure out of kilter.

Acquisition, too, served not only as a motivator but also as a purpose of life. In our own society, acquisition reached its fullest expression in the accumulation of wealth. (When you ask, "What's Mr. Jones worth?," there's no doubt about what you mean.) Students have been prepared for this by the use of symbols—gold stars, class listings, awards. Piling up honors, tangible or intangible, has had the effect of divorcing the student from his own feelings, his own being. A man's worth, it might be noted, is measured by things *outside* himself. These things are best measured by symbols (words, figures), which helps account for the dominance of symbols over personal feelings in Western civilization.

A society that encourages competition and acquisition is almost sure to encourage aggression as well. This may be seen on a national scale in the drive to acquire territory, wealth or status—especially by means of war or colonization. Preparing young men in the behaviors needed for these activities has become perhaps the most powerful shaper of education—and of life's purpose. Most of the utopian writers have acknowledged this primacy. Recent educational theorists have not; but conflict is there nonetheless, rooted deeply not only in educational practices, but in our language itself. It provides, in fact, one of the most pervasive metaphors through which we apprehend reality. We find ourselves engaged in a "war on poverty," a "battle against discrimination," a "mobilization for peace." I once tried to produce a long journalistic project without the use of a single conflict metaphor. It was not easy.

The history of mankind, and of education, has been a history of *men*. Thus, as Charles W. Ferguson has pointed out in *The Male Attitude,* it has been a chronicle of war, conquest, politics, hot competition and abstract reasoning. "What survives in the broad account of the days before the modern era," Ferguson writes, "is a picture of a humankind full of hostility and inevitable hate."

The male bias of education explains a great deal. In order for young men to bear the conditions of war or colonization, it was necessary that they reduce their imagination and self-awareness to a minimum. One could best live in an alien land governing an alien race or fight to the death against an impersonal foe by conceiving oneself as an instrument of something other than oneself. This trick of detachment has been taught in many ways. Stereotyped behaviors were trained by close-order drill on the parade ground and instructional drill in the classroom. Slogans justified the behaviors. "To die for Rome is noble" said more for Rome than for the Roman soldier. Team games helped submerge and repudiate individual feelings. If it is true that the battle of Waterloo was won on the playing fields of Eton, it is also true that some of the players' sensibilities were lost there.

Concentration on technical proficiency has become one of the very best ways to avoid awareness of self. The swordsman in a duel or the jet pilot in a dogfight generally is more concerned with his technique than with the survival of his own physical person. Detachment from self reaches an extreme in the test pilot. Facing imminent death, his interest remains focused on his flight instruments. Millions have heard the voices of astronauts (test pilots all), calm and mechanical in the face of epic dangers. Courage? Yes, but also detachment, divorce from the self. These things can be taught. I remember a few episodes from my own pilot days in World War II. I later wondered at my "lack of fear." Once, while instructing in B-25s, I let my student get too close to the plane landing in front of us. A few feet off the ground, we were caught in the preceding plane's propwash; our right wing began sinking. I took the controls, applied left aileron, then full left rudder. The wing kept sinking. It seemed inevitable that it would hit the ground, that the plane would cartwheel and explode. I could visualize all of this and could hear my inner voice saying, quite calmly and with a certain irony, "I'm going to die." But these considerations were extremely distant and of little interest. What held me spellbound was the technical problem the situation presented. The rather unusual measure of adding right throttle finally brought the wing up just before it touched the ground. We climbed back to altitude, I handed the controls over to the student and we went on practicing landings.

Because of this and other wartime episodes, I am in a poor position to criticize the educational procedures that helped me operate successfully while remaining coolly detached from my own deepest feelings—standing at attention for hours in the July Alabama sun in flagrant disregard of the body's urgent messages; learning that "there are only three answers to a superior officer in this man's Air Corps, 'Yes, sir,' 'No, sir,' and 'No excuse, sir' "; practicing in-flight emergency procedures over and again, until they become not merely automatic but entirely impersonal. No, I cannot fault these measures when used in preparation for war, for the precarious conquest of the physical world or for the subduing of alien peoples. For such purposes, they are quite apt. I can wonder, though, at the extent to which they have shaped the entire educational enterprise, for boys and girls alike. Wartime aviation cadet training was nothing more than prep school exaggerated, and the prep school has long remained a model for the "quality" public school.

"Right answers," specialization, standardization, narrow competition, eager acquisition, aggression, detachment from the self. Without them, it has seemed, the social machinery would break down. Do not call the schools cruel or unnatural for furthering what society has demanded. The reason we now need radical reform in education is that society's demands are changing radically. It is quite safe to say that the human characteristics now being inculcated will not work much longer. Already they are not only inappropriate, but destructive. If education continues along the old tack, humanity sooner or later will simply destroy itself.

To take one example, the narrow competition, eager acquisition and aggression clustered around the manufacture, marketing and purchasing of automobiles in the U.S. have resulted in ever larger and more powerful internal-combustion engines. Dr. Philip Leighton, Professor of Chemistry, Emeritus of Stanford University, has calculated that just one modern American car consumes well over a thousand times as much oxygen as does a person. Worse yet, Dr. Leighton writes, "to carry off the exhaust gases, and dilute them to harmless concentrations, requires from five to ten million times as much air as does the driver. In other words, just one automobile, moving along a Los Angeles County freeway, needs as much air to disperse its waste products as do all the people in the County for breathing." The supply of oxygen in the earth's atmosphere is huge, but not unlimited. If the spread of the internal-combustion engine continues at its present rate all over the world, and if the oxygen-producing greenery keeps getting chopped down (to make space for roads, among other things), a time may come when there is simply not enough natural, uncontaminated air to support life.

And this is only one of many ways man is swiftly arranging his own destruction. Mere existence in the largest cities is becoming almost unendurable, even for the most affluent. Air pollution from the cities is reaching out and damaging forest greenery in distant mountain ranges. The most beautiful lakes and streams are being poisoned. Lovely hills are being leveled for monotonous house sites. The whole earth is being polluted: the bodies of seals, penguins, skuas and fish in the Antarctic, remote from the source of the poisoning, have been discovered to contain DDT.

"No man is an Island" and "All men are brothers" may have been theoretical statements before; but now, in the time of worldwide, interlocking, responsive, all-pervasive and powerful technology, they are urgent cries for self-preservation. The region-wide power blackouts of recent years have given us striking reminders of our interdependence. During the first great Eastern blackout, people in New York City found themselves walking down the streets singing with strangers, touching one another. They were reaching for the future. To die for Rome—or any other state—is no longer noble. It is too easy to take the whole world down with you. The H-Bomb is brotherhood's most decisive seal. Peripheral wars, ever more wasteful and frustrating, may go on for years to come. But WAR is through. What justification, then, is there for continuing those educational procedures that prepare the young for the conditions of gross conflict? Even on the most vigilantly maintained first line of national defense, one may now find young air force officers sitting at desks in underground silos studying for advanced degrees as they baby-sit their nuclear-tipped missiles.

But how about test pilots? Won't we need cool, detached, icy-eyed young men to complete the conquest of the universe? Perhaps not. Already, the most advanced aircraft are almost totally automated, just as will be the spaceships of the future. Putting men in those U.S. and Russian moon vehicles may turn out to have been, in the scientific community's own frame of reference, a silly salute to the past. I proposed in Chapter III that valuable by-products in the way of new perceptions and altered states of consciousness may reward our efforts at manned space flights. But I doubt if *those* rewards have been considered by the "practical" men who must justify the enormous cost of supporting human life in space. Many of them, I know, believe we would have done well to concentrate on much less expensive robot devices with hypersensitive sensors to do our moon exploring for us.

In any case, the age of man as a component—whether of a pyramid-building gang or a space system—is just about over. The future will require that men behave in *none* of the ways thus far noted. A world in which everyone will be in touch needs people in touch with themselves. Where the actions of one can drastically affect the lives of others far distant, it will be crucially important that each person master the skill of feeling what others feel. This skill, more than new laws or new politics, will soon become crucial to the survival of the race. Such empathy is possible only in one deeply aware of his own feelings. The future will very likely judge nothing less appropriate than detached, fragmented, unfeeling men. Such men have done their work. They have fought wars, built empires. But war no longer makes much sense in anybody's terms, and empires soon will be found only in the infinitely rich and varied common countryside of humanity. In a new quest, on a globe newly linked and painfully sensitive to the most distant disturbances, men who conceive of themselves as impersonal instruments can easily become instruments of destruction.

One of the first tasks of education, then, is to return man to himself; to encourage rather than stifle awareness; to educate the emotions, the senses, the so-called autonomic systems; to help people become truly responsive and therefore truly responsible.

Narrow competition, eager acquisition and the aggression that accompanies them—so essential to the Civilized life of the past—already have become inappropriate in most cases and soon may be disastrous. It is hard to find anyone who has thought seriously about the future who does not agree that these activities should be reduced. Many of the futurists, however, believe they are so deeply ingrained in "human nature" that the best we can do is divert them to less dangerous uses—sports, mercantile competition and the like. William James sought the moral equivalent of war. Modern ethnologists anthropomorphize animals, then animalize people. They speak of animals "discharging" their "anger," then go on to assume that every human being has within him an inevitable, fixed "quantity" of aggression that somehow must be "discharged."

This is not so. As previously argued, the lower animals do most of their learning over species-long spans, very little during the lifetime of any single animal. Changing their DNA-mediated learning would take many, many generations. People, on the other hand, do the great majority of their learning during the lifetime of each individual. The chief repository of human learning is not DNA, but society. Look there, if you will, for the seat of aggression. And even there the learning is far from perfect. Anyone who thinks that man is "naturally" aggressive should visit an infantry training school, where the most ingenious, desperate measures are needed to turn young Americans into aggressive killers. (Typical sign in the Fort Ord, California, training area: "THE SPIRIT OF THE BAYONET IS TO KILL.") But the measures are never altogether successful. Even when killing is socially sanctioned and highly rewarded, even when it may save the soldiers' own lives, many GIs never fire their rifles. During the Korean War, studies show, only one out of four fired during battle.

No, man is not "naturally" aggressive. "Instincts" are not *needed* to explain those aggressions which do exist. Even if man had not a trace of instinctive aggression, the conditions of Civilized living would require that he learn it. As these conditions change, so will man. The questions are: Will he change fast enough, or will the transition be too rough, too abrupt? And how can education ease the transition?

The first thing schools can do to reduce narrow competition, eager acquisition and aggression is to stop teaching them. Grades, tests, prizes, honors have proven woefully inadequate as motivators for learning, even at the height of the Civilized Epoch. It has been previously argued, in fact, that competition was used in the schools not really to help students learn other subjects, but to teach competition itself, to further specialization and standardization. When learning becomes truly rewarding for its own sake—and this goal has been given lip service for centuries—then narrow competition will be seen for what it is: irrelevant to the learning process and damaging to the development of free-ranging, lifelong learners.

Eager acquisition and aggression may seem more difficult to reduce. Thus far, the emotions and actions associated with them have been highly reinforcing. With life's rewards lodged outside the self, the acquisition of extraneous tangibles or intangibles has quite naturally been synonymous with success. And, under some circumstances, the behaviors and affective states associated with aggression can be most desirable. The blood runs fast, the senses sharpen, the veil of the commonplace falls away; a man can transcend himself.

Punishing eager acquisition and aggression has never really worked. It has created more scars than cures. It has left a legacy of resentment against social controllers who would quell in others what they themselves live by. Neither punishment nor diversion gives answers to this problem in education. Acquisition will slow when technology creates a condition of plenty rather than the usual deprivation for all. Aggression will quiet down when aggressiveness stops being reinforced.

Still, a faster, more specific, more positive remedy is needed to reduce aggression as well as competition and acquisition. The remedy already is available. It appears to us in the form of an alternative reinforcer that will stir the blood and senses, that will make aggression merely uninteresting. It is joy, delight, ecstasy, the ancient, potent cure so long feared by Civilization, now so specifically and obviously prescribed. Joy resides *within* the self and is the most relevant of reinforcers.

Just as many people consider peace simply the absence of war, others think of peacefulness as the absence of aggressiveness. But that is seeking substance in a vacuum. To oppose war or racial hatred by signing petitions and marching in protest may be useful. But those who really want to end these evils might better spend their energy in *building* situations that are more engrossing, that elicit more of the human potential, that excite the ecstasy in humankind. And those who really want to reduce aggression of all kinds may seek not to work out more punishments against it, but to *replace* it by creating the conditions of ecstasy. The person who has learned to seek and find intrinsic joy has no time, no desire for aggression. Humanity's new situation suggests not that "to die for Rome is noble," but that "to delight for Rome is noble."

The purpose of life? Schools for what? Words can never answer. Mankind's moments of passage are especially hard on language, and one is often tempted these days to concede the impossibility of handling new things with old words. One response has been intentional oversimplification: The purpose of life is to reproduce your kind, to serve society and to glorify God. The last portion of the statement may be redundant, for organized religions generally find a way (regardless of gospel or doctrine) to make serving society and glorifying God synonymous.

And then the question arises as to how to serve a society that will no longer *need* human components to keep it running, to prop it up almost moment by moment. One answer keeps coming to mind, an artless phrase from a BBC television special about California and a vision of the future. According to the narrator, in a future without work in the usual sense, people's main function might be not to get ahead or to accumulate wealth, but "to sing and dance and interact."

This audacious oversimplification resonates, but it also misleads. There is something about it and perhaps about all the musings in this chapter that might give an impression of passivity, of the purely negative aspects of reform: we must, for our own safety, turn from the excitements of competition, acquisition and aggression to a sort of idyllic, inward-turning ecstasy, a sort of pallid paradise. This is not at all what I have in mind. The emerging mode of life promises to be so challenging, so vivid, so intense as to render the old life extremely dull. The end of "job" means the end of the eight-hour day and the beginning of the twenty-four-hour day. Lifelong learning, lifelong creative change, is an exhilarating and dangerous endeavor that will require far more human intensity and courage than the old modes.

Nor will the new life be predominantly inward-turning. In a highly responsive, richly interconnected world, all of us—choose to or not—will be involved in building and constantly rebuilding a world community. Technologically, all things we can conjure up eventually will be possible. If we choose to control the weather anywhere, we will affect the weather everywhere. If we choose to leave it alone, that is also a choice. There is no escape from the challenge, the most awesome in this planet's history: Unless we can turn back the technological clock, we shall be forced to become—are becoming—co-creators of the world.

The personal and interpersonal challenges (by no means separate from the technological) are no less awesome. Freed from the hunter's struggle for survival, freed from the Civilized man's incumbency as specialized component, the human race can explore for the first time what it really means to be human. This quest will not be restricted to a small minority of seekers or holy men; it will be a pilgrimage by the millions, a search for the billion manifestations of increased human capacity. It will not be easy or restful, this journey into *terra incognita*. Without clear maps, without safe travel instructions, without comforting exhortations, we can only follow delight like a hound on a trail.

We cannot guess what the distant future will ask of its schools, but perhaps we can step far enough in the future to see what our children *already* need. Schools for what?

● To learn the commonly-agreed-upon skills and knowledge of the ongoing culture (reading, writing, figuring, history and the like), to learn it joyfully and to learn that all of it, even the most sacred "fact," is strictly tentative.
● To learn how to ring creative changes on all that is currently agreed upon.
● To learn delight, not aggression; sharing, not eager acquisition; uniqueness, not narrow competition.
● To learn heightened awareness and control of emotional, sensory and bodily states and, through this, increased empathy for other people (a new kind of citizenship education).

● To learn how to enter and enjoy varying states of consciousness, in preparation for a life of change.
● To learn how to explore and enjoy the infinite possibilities in relations between people, perhaps the most common form of ecstasy.
● To learn how to learn, for learning—one word that includes singing, dancing, interacting and much more—is already becoming the main purpose of life.

In the next two chapters, it is shown that these generalities of today will become specifics for tomorrow. They may seem to lead far from the school in which your child is now enrolled. And yet, in the deepest sense, they spring from the original American impulse toward hope and individual fulfillment. They spring, too, from a personal journey that began in an "ordinary" U.S. public school some thirteen years ago.

The fall of 1955 was a difficult time for American teachers. It was two years before the Russian sputnik was to go up and bring down a deluge of criticism on U.S. schoolmen; but already a vague discontent was in the air. This atmosphere encouraged a band of critics to launch attacks upon the educational establishment. Almost every national periodical had its own "expert." Most of them followed the Basic Education line; that is, they scathingly attacked teachers and "educationists" while offering a curious remedy for all of education's ills: "Go back"—back to the three Rs, back to phonics, back to tough, no-nonsense subject-matter drill, back to McGuffey's Readers.

Against this backdrop, I found myself assigned to produce a lengthy magazine feature on what my editor called "the plight of the teacher in America." The assignment offered all the freedom and prerogatives a journalist could wish. There were no preconditions or preconceptions. I could travel anywhere in the country I liked, take as long as I needed, call on any expert for consultation or for authorship of part of the feature.

Expert I was not, never having written a word on the subject of education, never having even visited a classroom except as a parent with daughters in the second and third grades. Aware of this lack, I plunged into the assignment, reading as much as I could of what had been written on the subject during the five preceding years, meeting with leading educators and their detractors. I found that my lack of expertise, far from being a handicap, was an advantage. In a year when most education writers carried axes to grind, my naïveté pleased everyone I interviewed.

The assignment captured me. I became totally involved. Dropping any notion of calling in outside help, I went ahead with plans to do all the writing myself. I would depend heavily on a picture story about one teacher. Through the teacher's day-by-day experiences, photographer Charlotte Brooks and I would try to illuminate the matters under debate in a way that would transcend diatribe and expertise. So we set out across the midlands of Illinois, visiting medium-sized schools in medium-sized towns on days when nothing out of the ordinary was happening, seeking one teacher who might, in some respect, represent a million more.

We came into Decatur, Illinois, before the end of harvest and we were still there when the snows were falling. Garfield School was an old, gloomy, blocklike structure of the general kind you have seen or imagined a thousand times. Its staff was neither the best nor the worst I had encountered. And the second-grade classroom presided over by a young second-year teacher named Carolyn Wilson was, on the surface, like any number of others. But it was here we decided to stay, to risk our whole project on the premise that the "ordinary" events in that room were not ordinary at all.

At first, we perceived only a fraction of what was happening. Then we began to realize that twenty-eight children represented twenty-eight little dramas exploding around us at every moment. Perceiving, we were overwhelmed. We were tumbled in a surf of impressions. Charlotte would focus on one situation and then, before she could click the shutter, something would happen on the periphery of her vision and she would whirl around to capture a moment already gone. We became obsessed with the lives in that room. After school, we talked of nothing else, endlessly pondering the complex maze of interaction between children and children, between children and teacher. We learned. Charlotte's camera became more accurate. She was there at the high moments. Still, it was all too swift. The click of the camera lagged a fraction of a second behind the action. We both felt as if we were swimming endlessly against a current.

Gradually, as the weeks passed, we became part of Carolyn Wilson's class. We found ourselves sitting on the floor among the children. They didn't seem to consider it strange. We got onto their verbal level and into their lives. Everything began working. What had been hard became easy. The click of Charlotte's camera made perfect accompaniment to the action, pizzicato accents in a ballet. Carolyn rushed to the lavatory with a boy who was about to vomit. Somehow Charlotte was there ahead of him, in position, camera focused. And one afternoon just after lunch, she caught an elfin, yellow-haired boy in the very act of learning. It made an unforgettable sequence. I was to describe it as one of "those magic moments when knowledge leaps across the gap like a spark, and a child flings up his hand, exulting, 'I know. *I know!*'"

In Carolyn Wilson's class, the educational haggling in the periodicals simply faded into irrelevance. How could anyone smugly prescribe "intellectual rigor" for Sherryl, whose parents had just separated, leaving her bewildered and half-crippled by anxiety? What did "concentration on subject-matter content" mean to Harold, who sometimes came to school tired and hungry? Charlotte and I were appalled at the teacher's situation. Society had carelessly heaped Herculean tasks upon her—and she just didn't have the tools, the techniques, the environment to do what was required. The solutions offered by the Basic Education writers seemed not only inadequate, but malicious.

We visited other towns, other classrooms. I looked into educational experiments and investigated the critics' main charges. Something obviously was wrong with the schools, but it was certainly not what the critics were saying. I completed my assignment in a fury of admiration for teachers. Caught up in impossible situations, they seemed to me the real heroes and heroines of the times. They needed more understanding and help, not self-righteous slander.

These feelings were revealed in the feature, which appeared under the general title "What Is a Teacher?," and included pictures, text and "A Magna Carta for Teachers." By the time it came out in *Look*'s February 21, 1956, issue, I was already at work on something else and never dreamed of doing any more stories on education. But "What Is a Teacher?" would not release me so easily. It struck some sort of national chord and quickly stirred up the concomitants of "success" that have become so familiar in novels and movies—showers of letters and wires, requests for reprints, awards, translation into many languages. So, I often found myself in school again in the years that followed, reporting on gifted children, school boards, superintendents, slum schools, vocational education, testing, the teaching of writing, programmed instruction and the like. I worked hard at not becoming an expert. Each story, I figured, would be best approached as if my first.

But I moved away from "What Is a Teacher?" I became increasingly concerned not with the way things are, but how they could be. New experiments showed how woefully we had underrated children's ability to learn. New techniques to help children learn—just what teachers needed, it seemed to me—became available. And I became increasingly involved with education outside of journalism.

I guess it was inevitable I would fall out of love with that first story. There is a modern disease of detachment and despair that has infected many of our most noted intellectuals; the symptoms include a morbid fear of enthusiasm and an inability to perceive hope in any situation. The disease is highly contagious. I was not immune. "What Is a Teacher?"—enthusiastic, hopeful, emotional— began to seem embarrassingly naïve and starry-eyed to me. I found myself omitting it when people asked for reprints of my past educational stories. I wanted to be as full of existential despair as the next writer.

That was some years ago. I hope I have been cured. A certain naïveté is prerequisite to all learning. A certain optimism is prerequisite to all action. When a nation's best minds desert all hope and decry all enthusiasm, they leave the nation susceptible to nihilism and anarchy. When they refuse to be committed, they leave commitment to those who would destroy, not build, those who would go back, not forward. Existential despair is the ultimate copout. I'll have no more of it.

And now I leaf through a copy of "What Is a Teacher?". Thirteen years is archeological time in the field of magazines. One of the pages is torn. The pictures seem faded. But the moments are vivid and the thesis seems right. I do not deny my enthusiasm. A yellow-haired boy flings up his hand. A tearful boy with a crew cut pulls away from Carolyn Wilson's embrace, resisting forgiveness. A doleful little girl nestles in the curve of Carolyn's body. And, on page after page, the teacher is there, struggling cheerfully against impossible odds, bolstered by unsubstantiated hope, saying, "There is good in every child."

I reach for the future from Carolyn Wilson's classroom (though there will be no classrooms). I borrow my spirit of hope from her and the hundreds of teachers I have known (though there will be no teachers as we now think of them). And if my school of the future seems a radical departure, it is only because the human potential I have found in schools like Garfield in Decatur, Illinois, demands that we now take radical measures.

ANYONE WHO TRIES *to draw the future in hard lines and vivid hues is a fool. The future will never sit for a portrait. It will come around a corner we never noticed, take us by surprise. And yet, foolishly, I cannot deny a vision born of indignation and hope. George Sand has called indignation at what is wrong in humanity one of the most passionate forms of love. If this is so, hope for something better may be love of a more enduring sort. Kennedy School in Santa*

8. VISITING DAY, 2001 A. D.

Fe, New Mexico, exists not in the blazing immediacy of the twenty-first century, but in the indignation and hope of today. If it should sound like science fiction, do not be misled. Everything there is technically feasible. We don't really have to wait until the year 2001; it is only people, their habits, their organizations that may take so long to move. The alternatives, real alternatives, exist now.

A spring morning, 2001 A.D. It is visiting day, but not in any special sense; every day is visiting day. We are among those parents who frequently drop by Kennedy School when our children are there or even on those rare days when they choose not to attend. We go not through any sense of duty (though I guess that old-fashioned word would apply to what we feel for our children), but out of sheer fascination. In fact, there's a certain amount of kidding among members of our adult learning group about how much time we spend in our children's early-school— "lifting ideas for our own projects."

We catch a glimpse of the school before driving our electric down the ramp and into the underground parking lot. The sight, as always, pleases us—gleaming geodesic domes and translucent tentlike structures scattered randomly among graceful trees; a large grassy playfield encircled with flowers; all of it a testament to the foresight of community planners who set aside the land decades ago. Educators in the great strip cities haven't had it so easy. Some of them have had to build vertically; others are still engaged in lengthy negotiations for enough land for a few trees and flowers.

We walk up a ramp to an entrance. Two postgrads, an eleven-year-old boy and girl, welcome us with hugs and kisses. The girl finds our electronic identification devices on a large board, and we clip them to our clothing. The boy gives each of us a flower—a large orchid-like bloom, orange speckled with deep red, for my wife; a lavender rose for me—the products, we know, of botanical experiments by a group of six- to ten-year-olds. We thank our hosts with another embrace and stroll through a grove of oaks toward the Basics Dome, where we may find our three-year-old, Sally. Even if we knew Sally was somewhere else, we'd probably go there first anyway.

On the way, we pass children of various ages in various states of consciousness. Some are walking aimlessly, alone or in small groups, perhaps toward some destination, perhaps not. Others are running. We notice a group of around seven of the older children with two of the educators in impassioned encounter near one of the biggest trees. Almost in our pathway sits a little girl with long black hair and dark skin—probably of Mexican-Indian extraction. Her enormous black eyes seem to hold a powerful dream, and we tiptoe around her, so as not to disturb her inner voyaging. But she looks up and, for a moment, shares with us something mysterious.

A total of some 800 children between three and ten are enrolled in Kennedy, but on a typical morning only about 600 (around seventy-five of each chronological age) are on the school grounds. Most of the educational environments are in operation from eight in the morning until six in the afternoon. Children can come when and if they please; there's no problem at all if parents wish to take their children on extended trips or simply keep them home for something that's going on there.

While the children are on the school grounds, they are *absolutely* free to go and do *anything* they wish that does not hurt someone else. They are *free learners.* The italics belong to Will Hawthorne, Kennedy's Principal Educator. The free-learning concept has, of course, been accepted for years all over the U.S. Almost every educator gives it lip service, and the overwhelming majority of them follow it to one degree or another. Will, however, lives and breathes it.

"*Everything* starts there," he tells parents. "Until we had the free learner, we really didn't know *anything* about education. The free learner built Kennedy School." Will is a student of educational history and has created several experiential tapes on the development of the concept. "This feisty old radical named A. S. Neill started a place called Summerhill in England in 1924," Will tells parents. "Children were relatively free, but there was no systematic attempt to create learning environments, to find out what human beings really were capable of. There was no real vision of the human potential. Summerhill was mostly a *reaction* to the incredibly inefficient and cruel teaching system of the day. Unfortunately, too, it was tied to the dogma of the then voguish Freudian psychology, with its static and limiting views of the human personality. Still, there was a remarkable interest in Neill's books that reflected a widespread though unfocused hunger for educational reform.

"It was not until the late 1960s and early 1970s that real free-learning schools began springing up here and there, and it was only then that educators could start learning about education. The first such schools were crude affairs. For one thing, the educators of that day found it very difficult to give up the idea of teacher-led classes at certain periods. So—even though the children were ranging freely all over the building—you had someone walking around at given times ringing a bell to announce the beginning of, say, 'math class' for anyone who cared to attend. If the class was made interesting enough—a heroic endeavor under the circumstances—quite a few kids would come. But the enormous *inefficiency* and the *expense* of the 'class and teacher' situation became more and more apparent. Learning environments could be created, it was discovered, for constant operation and full utilization, always available for children and yet always amenable to modification by educators.

"Among the earliest such environments were simple, paper-and-pencil self-instructional programs, mostly in such basic subjects as reading, spelling, figuring and the like. Most of them were terribly linear, unimaginative and single-tracked. But they did their job in demonstrating that the free-learning situation was feasible, even in terms of the strictly limited training offered in that day. Not only that, they freed some teachers to become educators, and these fledgling educators began asking themselves questions on what education was all about. Free learners were there to help give them the answers.

"At around the same time, another development moved in from an entirely different direction. Several large corporations started pushing Computer-Assisted Instruction (CAI). The computer learning programs were at first even more limited and stereotyped than the paper-and-pencil programs. And the learning consoles were mounted, of all places, in 'classrooms.' Children had to come to them at certain fixed periods and sit there under the 'guidance' of 'teachers.'

"You know, this is one of the most difficult things for our children to recreate experientially. I mean, the whole business of classrooms and teachers. They can conceptualize it. They've seen the historical films. But, during their history-drama sessions, they rarely can truly get the *feeling* we know existed then. When the child playing teacher forces the children playing students to sit still while teacher gives a long blackboard demonstration, the students find it very hard to get the *feeling* of being bored, distracted, or squirming and hoping for time to pass. Many of them simply go into a relaxed, serene state of semimeditation, enjoying the whole situation immensely. The child serving as history-drama coordinator senses this, naturally enough, and stops the drama amid much laughter and confusion. The fact that children once had to get *permission* to go and urinate is even harder for them to understand.

"Anyhow, the computer and the free school were destined for marriage, and it didn't take them long to get together. By the mid-1970s, most of what was called 'Computer-Assisted Instruction' was being applied in free-learning situations. Immediate economies and efficiencies were realized in terms the Systems Engineering people of the time could understand. The system was, in fact, *too* efficient for the educational goals then envisaged. Children could finish everything too fast and too easily. 'Homework' went right out of the window, creating dismay and anxiety, strangely enough, among many parents. The Great National School Debate of the middle and late 1970s concerned what to do with all the extra time gained by the new mode of learning. The question generally was stated in this fashion: 'What is the province of education?' The answer was simple: 'Everything.'

"During the 1970s, most schools spent a great deal of time with encounter groups for children and educators. These served to educate the emotions and to break down the old protective, defensive patterns of relating. They helped open people to all sorts of capacities they barely realized they had. Gradually the encounter mode became a part of everything the learners did, and it was no longer necessary to set up these groups as such.

"At the same time, educators were finding out that computer-mediated programs could be constructed to encourage uniqueness rather than sameness in learners. In fact, by tying to the ongoing program referents from a memory bank consisting of all the learner's past responses, the learner's distinctness from all other learners could be rapidly increased. Too rapidly, it seemed to some educators.

"The programs still were narrow, concerned with one 'subject' at a time—in other words, they were *programs*. Then, gradually, they evolved into what we now call 'dialogues.' It started when programmers began adding novelty and surprise through what they at first termed 'extraneous material.' For example, material about astronomy would pop up in programs on Eastern philosophy. Soon, they began realizing that what they were adding was by no means extraneous. Far from it, cross-matrix learning increased the central nervous system's capability for making connections, as well as enhancing mastery of any given subject. The early 1980s were fascinated with Cross-Matrix Stimulus and Response (CMSR). Naturally enough, the cross-matrix linkage started out quite teleologically, with the dialoguers seeking 'reasons' for their connections. But 'reasons' were found to be unduly limiting. Random retrieval through a central school computer made it possible to bring material up from the general cultural data bank, from the learner's own past responses and from the discontinuous symbolic storage to create displays that were anything but teleological.

"It was about this time, too, that dialoguers began conceiving the displays not only as learning aids, but as artistic creations in their own right. It occurred to them that the two—art and learning—really were one. That was still in the period when the displays were presented on old-fashioned cathode-ray television screens mounted in front of each learner. The art-and-learning movement was given a tremendous push around 1985, when the hologrammatic-conversion problem was solved for mass production. Laser-type projection created images of unimagined brightness and resolution—*moving* images that seemed to hang in midair, in dimensions that somehow outshone reality.

"An even more important development of the 1980s was the application of Ongoing Brain-wave Analysis (OBA) to Computer-Assisted Dialogue (CAD). The experiments of such pioneers as Kamiya and Adey had already shown that it was possible, through computer analysis, to identify the brain-wave patterns not only of certain general states of consciousness but also those associated with effective short-term memory. Certain experimenters began attaching brain-wave sensors to learners' earphones, so that their wave patterns could be fed directly into the computer for ongoing analysis and immediate influence of the dialogue. In this way, the learning process could march along much more swiftly and surely, and the number of overt motor responses—speech or key pressing, for example—required of the learner could be greatly reduced. If the learner was responding neurologically, the dialogue could move on. His general state of consciousness could also influence the dialogue.

"It took a few years for OBA to spread to most of the nation's schools. By that time, of course, musical-rhythmic sound had become a key matrix in CMSR. As the Hindus say, *Nada-Brahma-,* Sound Is God. And with sound responding to a learner's innermost states, a sort of cosmic counterpoint was born. The 1990s were a period of consolidation of the basic techniques, with breathtaking advances in the state of the art not only in Computer-Assisted Dialogue, but in a great number of educational environments."

Will Hawthorne's ebullience turns to caution only when the matter of Direct Brain-wave Manipulation (DBM) comes up. "First of all," he says, "it will be many years before DBM has anywhere near the subtlety and specificity of CAD through the usual sense channels. Then, too, I just don't like the idea of bypassing the senses, the sources of ever-present joy. No, if I have anything to say about it, there won't be any Kennedy children wearing those cumbersome DBM electrode helmets until I've seen a lot more data, especially concerning sensory side effects."

Some parents and children consider Will hopelessly conservative in this matter. But one visit to the Basics Dome explains why he is reluctant to "go inside." My wife and I find our pace quickening as we approach the most active and spectacular learning environment at Kennedy. We go in through one of three tunnel-like entrances and emerge near the center of a great dome lit only by the glow of laser learning displays that completely surround us on the dome's periphery. Sitting or sprawled on cushions scattered on the floor are other parents and older children who have come just for the experience, in addition to the little children waiting their turns at the learning consoles. We settle down and open our senses.

No matter how many times you visit the Basics Dome, its initial effect is literally stunning. It takes a while for the nervous system to begin processing; first, you have to surrender to the overwhelming sensory bombardment that comes from every side. There are, around us, forty learning consoles, at each of which is seated a child between the ages of three and seven, facing outward toward the learning displays. Each child sits at a keyboard, essentially less complex than that of an old-fashioned typewriter, but fitted with a number of shifts so that almost every symbol known to human cultures can be produced. The child's learning display, about ten feet square, is reflected from the hologram-conversion screen that runs all the way around the inner surface of the dome. The image appears to stand out from the screen in sometimes startling colors and dimensions. The screen is slightly elevated above the child's horizontal eye level so that everyone in the dome, by turning all the way around, can view all of the learning displays. Each display joins the one on either side of it, so that the total effect is panoramic. And each has its own set of stereo speakers, joining in a panorama of sound.

There are almost always children waiting for each console. A small electronic tablet on the back of each chair shows the name of the child in the chair and the number of minutes he has left in his learning session. The amount of time allowed for each session varies; it is calculated electronically according to the total number of children waiting in the dome, but it is never less than twenty minutes. Young children entering the dome shop around for consoles that have few or no other children waiting and that have the shortest time to go. The child assures his waiting place simply by touching the tablet with his electronic identification device (EID); a receiver picks up the information and the child's name appears at the bottom of the list on the tablet.

When a child takes the chair to begin learning, another radio receiver senses his presence through his EID and signals the central learning computer to plug in that particular child's learning history. The child puts on his combination earphones and brain-wave sensors, so that OBA can become an element in the dialogue. (Some schools use the brain-wave pattern, much in the manner of a fingerprint, to identify the learner.) Once the computer picks up the child's ongoing brain-waves, it immediately begins reiterating (in drastically foreshortened form) his last learning session. The child watches his most recent lesson reeling by on his display. If he wants to continue where he left off last time, he holds down his "yes" key until the reiteration is finished. If not, he presses "no," and the computer begins searching for other material appropriate to the child's level of learning, material which is flashed onto the display until the child presses "yes." The "select" process generally takes less than two minutes. The dialogue then begins.

At any given time during the dialogue, five variables are at hand:

1. A full bank of the basic, commonly agreed-upon cultural knowledge, arranged in dialogue form. Most children go through the entire basics bank in the four years from age three through age six.

2. Basic material arranged in Cross-Matrix Stimulus and Response form. This material appears at random intervals along with the dialogued material, to provide novelty and surprise and to help the child learn to make those unexpected leaps which are so much a part of discovery.

3. The child's brain-wave pattern, analyzed in terms of general consciousness state and short-term memory strength.

4. The child's overt motor responses as typed on the keyboard or spoken into a directional microphone mounted on the console.

5. Communal Interconnect (CI). This is one of the very latest educational developments. Only a few of the nation's schools have it. Through CI, the material on one learning display sometimes influences and is influenced by the material on nearby displays. This makes the learning process far more communal. It also helps tie together all forty displays into a single learning-art object, enhancing learning

and appreciation, not only for the children at the consoles, but for the many spectators in the dome as well.

As soon as our senses become accustomed to the sounds and sights and smells in the dome, we look around for Sally. We are pleased to find her at one of the consoles. We move over to the side of the circle of spectators nearest her.

Sally, we notice on the electronic tablet on her chair, is only five minutes into her learning session. There is a Negro boy, probably six, on her left who is deep into a simple calculus session. On Sally's right, a girl of four or five is dialoguing about primitive cultures. Sally herself, as in her last several sessions, is concerned with simple language skills. It quickly becomes apparent that she has launched into a session on breaking her linguistic set. Standard spelling and syntax are generally learned during the first half of a child's third year of age. During the second half (where Sally is now) an equal or greater amount of time is spent trying out alternate forms. This leads eventually, after the basics are finished, to a key project: almost every child, working with friends, creates an entire new language before leaving Kennedy School.

We watch Sally's display, which now seems to be billowing with pink and lavender clouds. Gradually, the clouds take the shape of some kind of animal's face. Before I can make out what it is, I hear Sally saying "Cat" into her microphone. Almost instantly, a huge, grinning cat's face gathers form and the word "cat" appears at the bottom of the display. Then a written conversation begins between Sally and the Computer-Assisted Dialogue, with the words of each appearing on the display:

CAD: Can you think of an alternate spelling?
SALLY [*Typing*]: kat.

On the display, the giant cat face recedes and is transformed into a white Angora cat, surrounded by vibrating, jagged radial lines of many colors. A purring sound comes from the display.

CAD: How about another?
SALLY [*Pausing a moment*]: katte.

The purring becomes louder.

CAD: A cat is a kat is a katte.
SALLY [*Quickly*]: A katte is a kat is a cat.
CAD: Copy cat.
SALLY: Koppy kat.

There is a pause as the cat image gradually fades and the purring mingles with sweeping electronic music coming from the display on the left. As the dialogue goes on there between boy and CAD in the lovely visual symbols of calculus, a spinning wheel fills most of the display. Through its spokes, slender and glistening like the spokes of a bicycle wheel, may be viewed the rush of its motion—across grassy fields, deserts, down winding mountain roads. A ghostly image of the wheel appears on Sally's display, too, along with multicolored, dancing wave forms, related somehow to her brain waves. On the display at the right, an African pygmy with a blowgun stalks an unseen prey through dense jungle as the girl at the console carries on a voice-only dialogue with CAD. Suddenly Sally begins to type again:

SALLY: A cat hiss a kat hiss a katte.
CAD: WILD!!!

Sally's display explodes for a moment with dazzling bursts of color, then becomes the jungle of the girl at the right, in which may be seen the prey of the hunter, a leopard. A tentative, suspenseful drumming echoes back and forth between the two displays. The two girls turn to each other smiling, then Sally quickly starts typing:

SALLY: A tiger is a tigger./ A gunne has a trigger.

A moment after the last letter of Sally's couplet appears on her display, the jungle remains the same, but the leopard becomes a tiger and the pygmy becomes a white hunter of the early twentieth century, carrying a gun. The girl at the right snaps her head around at Sally, smiling, and Sally laughs delightedly.

CAD: Why not "leopard"?
SALLY: "Leopard" doesn't rime with "trigger."
CAD: Okay. How about some alternate spellings for "leopard"?
SALLY: That's easy. Leppurd.

Meanwhile, the girl at the right keeps talking to CAD and suddenly the tiger becomes a leopard, the white hunter, a pygmy again. The pygmy lifts his blowgun and with a sharp, explosive exhalation that echoes through the dome, sends a dart into the air. The display becomes a closeup of the dart coursing in slow motion across the girl's display, across Sally's and into the boy's at the left, disappearing in the hub of the spinning wheel. Another dart arches across the three displays, then another and another, sailing, soaring, starting always from different angles but ending invariably in the center of the boy's spinning wheel.

"Beautiful CI!" I hear my wife exclaim, and I notice

that several people are watching the sequence and listening to the rise and fall of the accompanying electronic music. I also see that the flight of the darts is beginning to influence displays even farther along the line. But the boy continues his calculus dialogue and Sally goes on, too:

CAD: "Leppurd" is good, but you don't have to stay with sound correspondence. Would you like to try something farther out?

Sally presses her "yes" key, then pauses before beginning to type:

SALLY: Leap-heart.
CAD: Nice. Do you want to do another?
SALLY: No.

The flying darts begin to fade. Gradually, Sally's display takes on the deep, rich, undulating plum purple that often characterizes the brain's alpha-wave pattern. Some of the gorgeous richness spills over onto the displays at either side. We know her eyes are closed. She is serene. It is one of education's more valuable moments. We, too, are serene. It is easy, in this setting, to share Sally's feelings. We also share the sheer delight of the educators who set up and constantly modify this learning environment. It is a kind of delight that was unknown to lecturers.

When Sally's session is finished, we walk with her out of the Basics Dome. We talk for a while, but soon she sees some of her friends and leaves us. They run off toward the thickest grove of trees to continue an animal game that may take them the rest of the day.

So we stroll from one place to another, looking (but not

too strenuously) for Johnny, our nine-year-old. If we were in a hurry to find him, it would be easy enough. We would merely go to the Central Dome and present one of our electronic identification devices to the ongoing scan, then read out Johnny's approximate present location. Every child wears an EID whenever he is on the school grounds, and the central computer continually tabulates how much time he spends in each educational environment. In addition, whenever the child is in dialogue with a CAD, his learning experience is stored in the computer. This allows Kennedy's educators, not only to keep track of each child's educational development with a minimum of effort, but also to evaluate the drawing power and effectiveness of each environment. The first principle of free learning is that if an environment fails to draw or to educate, it is the environment's, not the learner's, fault.

Visiting educators from educationally underdeveloped nations sometimes find it hard to understand that EID tracking serves not to enforce conformity, but just the opposite. In fact, "asymmetry" is highly valued. Will Hawthorne becomes quite excited when a young child resists the enticements of the Basics Dome for a year or two. Such a child may turn out to be so unique that much can be learned from him. And individual uniqueness is itself one of the main goals of the educational process.

Anyway, learning the basics, the commonly agreed-upon cultural stuff, is so sure and easy that there's never any worry about delay in starting it. It seems incredible to today's children that there ever was.

"I still find it hard to believe," Johnny sometimes says, "that people of Grandpa's generation spent *most* of their time in school learning just what the little kids learn in Basics."

"It's really true," my wife tells him. "They learned

much less. And they did spend almost all their school time working at it."

"*Working?*" Sally asks in amazement.

"Yes. *Really.* And there were all sorts of discussions and arguments about how to do it and every kind of agony you can imagine."

Even in my parents' day, the distinction between college and "real life" had begun to blur, with millions of people engaged in what was then called "adult education," and millions of students dropping in and out of school. The sealed-off four years that once were college began breaking up; no longer was it possible to keep the academy separate from the community. Increasingly, the university became a study-work-recreation center for everyone. It offered various types of "membership," ranging from full-time participation to subscription to a university news service received in the home on electronic consoles. The fast, effective flow of information via computer-mediated networks made decentralization possible, and the unwieldy giants of higher education began breaking down into smaller units.

At the same time, learning environments outside the traditional university proliferated and flourished. Laymen set up their own institutes, schools, research centers. Industries and businesses realized that their real business was learning and the spread of learning. The family unit, it came clear, was basically an educational unit. Parents began consciously designing the home as an environment in which to learn.

College degrees had become rather meaningless by the time I reached my teens: they were just too commonplace; there was so much learning going on outside of college; and the emphasis in education had turned from extrinsic to intrinsic satisfactions. The old hassles over admissions, processing and graduation had created the need for top-heavy administrative staffs. With these hassles greatly diminished, administration could be reduced, and educators and researchers could get on with education and research. Universities, unique and highly decentralized, still do exist, but not apart from the rest of the community. They are taking their place among a growing number and diversity of learning environments.

More and more communities, including Santa Fe, have begun limiting free, tax-supported education to the ages from three through ten. A sort of apprenticeship system is developing for older children. After ten, children can move from one learning environment to another, whether it be a formal school or not. Various financial arrangements are evolving, with the learner or his parents generally paying a small amount to the learning environment. After apprenticeship, the learner might receive pay for the same activity he previously had been paying for.

The Renaissance author of *The City of the Sun,* Tommaso Campanella, provided a curious piece of historical foresight when he imagined that "boys are accustomed to learn all the sciences, without toil and as if for pleasure; but in the way of history only until they are ten." If we read "history" as "all that is already known," and "science" as "research and lifelong learning," we may say that we are at last coming close to that utopian goal.

With Sally out of sight, we continue our casual search for Johnny. The Quiet Dome is smaller than the Basics Dome and made of a translucent, milky-white material. Perhaps Johnny will be there, practicing the omega-form meditation he has recently been learning. We leave our shoes in one of the racks that line the entrance and push our way in through three separate sets of heavy, sound-absorbing curtains. Inside, we step onto a spongy floor that floats free from the earth on hydraulic mounts.

Just as the Basics Dome shocks the senses with an initial overload of stimuli, the Quiet Dome shocks with the lack of them. All of the interior materials absorb sound, and batteries of deep, conelike sound deadeners line the inner wall six feet up all the way around. A number of nondirectional speakers pour out a gentle flood of white sound (like that of a distant waterfall) which suffuses the space, just as does the pale, directionless light. A faint odor of balsamic incense neutralizes the sense of smell. Everything is neutral, directionless, without dimension.

We look around for Johnny, but in vain. So we sit for a while amid scores of children and a few parents, shedding the exterior world like a superfluous garment. Almost immediately, a fantasy takes form in my consciousness. It is not easy to put into words. I am in a sort of column of force, slowly ascending to another level where I move into another column and so on. It is a delicious if somewhat awesome feeling, and I simply experience it for a while. Then I shift from an experiential to a problem-solving mode of consciousness. Perhaps I can apply the fantasy to a concept of interfamily communications. *Imagine that the family members exist on different levels; that they can communicate deeply only when they join, even temporarily, on a common level; that there is only a discrete number of "columns"—maybe only one—between each level; that the members cannot communicate while en route from level to level.* I go on conceptualizing, not really getting anywhere, but enjoying myself.

And then I get a strong signal—you might call it "extrasensory"—from my wife that she wants to go on looking for Johnny. I turn to her and nod and we exchange the rather knowing smile that sometimes celebrates this particular form of intimacy. We leave, stepping past children locked in silence and contemplation. While meditation is encouraged everywhere on the school grounds, especially outdoors among the trees and flowers, the Quiet Dome is available always, good weather or bad. Kennedy educators consider it necessary that the learner be free to retreat, to take a stand within himself. He can then reenter the world of active learning enriched by new inner connections.

We walk on to the Water and Body Domes. These domes are joined together about halfway up, creating two interconnected circular areas inside. One of the areas contains a free-form swimming pool; the dome above it slides open to the sun. The other area is a gymnasium and dance floor. The pool, we find, is fairly crowded with nude children. I comment on how many of the very youngest are in the water.

"Yes," my wife adds. "Will says that every single new three-year-old could swim by Christmas."

There are no adults in the pool—no "lifeguard," no "instructors." The older children take full responsibility for the younger, helping them learn to swim and otherwise handle themselves in the water. As Will points out, it would be practically impossible for any of the newcomers to drown. The older children have developed their empathy, their awareness of others, to a high state. There is no higher educational goal.

Over in the gym and dance area, two educators are always on hand to counsel learners about the all-important relationship between the body—its posture, tension, movements and coordination—to everything else in life and learning. A group of about ten children of various ages is dancing near the center of the floor. An educator watches as they express their feelings, in sequence, toward each member of the group, using physical movement only. When they finish, the educator will give verbal feedback on what has happened, if any child should ask. More important, he will help them pick up the feedback from their own bodies. He will help them realize how movement may alter perception.

Children at the far edge of the dome are learning to

control their muscle tension, blood pressure, heart rate, peristalsis and the like. They are aided in this by quite simple Body Feedback (BF) devices that have been in use for decades. To reduce muscle tension in the neck, for example, the child sits, attaches electrodes with suction cups on either side of the neck and puts on earphones. As the tension relaxes, the tone in his earphones becomes lower in pitch. The child merely concentrates on lowering the pitch. When he does so, the muscles are relaxed. Similar sound feedback is provided for each of the body functions being educated. Two eleven- or twelve-year-old postgrads monitor the BF devices and help children attach the electrodes or other sensors. The BF devices are equipped with automatic safety cutoffs so that the children cannot reach any bodily state that might be dangerous. Within rather wide limits, however, they are encouraged to experiment freely in bringing their functions under voluntary control. They are also encouraged to control the functions *without* BF as soon as possible. We notice a cluster of children doing just that, practicing the control of respiration and pulse rate while one of the body educators watches. It is through such exercises that each child learns to read his body as accurately and easily as he reads print. When this is possible, "psychosomatic" complaints are extremely unlikely.

We walk toward the playfield. On the way we pass several Discovery Tents—structures of translucent plastic erected on skeletal frameworks over lightweight plastic floors. The tents are provided with portable air conditioners. They are easily movable or convertible to a different shape. Their character is tentative, temporary.

As we stroll past, we can make out the shapes of children inside, but can't tell exactly what they are doing. Adults rarely enter Discovery Tents. An educator is responsible for each tent (sometimes one educator handles more than one tent), but he sees his function as setting up and constantly revising educational environments that will encourage children to make their own discoveries. For example, one educator handles both of the current Matter/Energy Manipulation projects, making sure the appropriate apparatus and "instructions" are available every day. He strives to create conditions that will stretch the learners' abilities without leaving them behind.

Only a few electronic or printed reference materials are needed inside the Discovery Tents. Every learner in the school, once he has finished enough of the Basics, is given a Remote Readout device through which he can query the Central Computer at any time. The device is slightly larger than an old-fashioned cigarette pack. It has a visual display screen large enough for several lines of type at the time or for small diagrams and pictures. It is fitted with a miniature microphone, slimmer than a pencil, and an earplug. The learner thus has voice access to the computer. He can also contact the educator in charge of the project. Most of the children, however, are reluctant to do so. They have found that the real joy of learning lies in finding out for themselves, either alone or in concert with other children.

When an educator has finished setting up a new project environment, he describes its possibilities on a display at the tent's entrance. Children of various ages wander in. They are electronically recognized through their EIDs, and their names appear under "Visiting" on the display at the entrance. If they should decide to become involved in the project, they touch their EIDs to an electrode beneath the display panel, and their names then appear under "Involved." When enough children for a given project have "signed up," the display announces, "Project filled.

Please try again later." Word about the ongoing projects always spreads; at particularly exciting ones you may find children checking several times daily to see if anyone has dropped out.

For several years now, one of the more popular events in the Discovery Tents has been the "Faraday Project," arranged by the Matter/Energy Manipulation educator. A tent is set up, insofar as possible, just like Michael Faraday's laboratory on the morning of August 29, 1831. All the appropriate excerpts from Faraday's notebooks dealing with the relationship between electricity and magnetism to that date are available to the children. Also provided are reports of other experimenters, notably Hans Christian Oersted, who had demonstrated that magnetism could be obtained from electricity. The equipment in the tent is primitive: wire, magnets, iron cores, batteries, a galvanometer. Nothing is available that was not available to Faraday. The learners' goal is the same as was his: "conversion of Magnetism into Electricity."

Faraday, in ten inspired days, not only accomplished his goal, but also found essentially all the laws that govern electromagnetic induction and built a working model of an electric dynamo. The children of Kennedy School start out with great advantages over Faraday. They know very well that magnetism *can* be made into electricity; most of them have a pretty good idea of how it is done. What is fascinating is to see just what a group of twelve to fifteen of the young ones (six- to eight-year-olds) come up with and how long it takes them. Often their experiments lack the elegance and economy of Faraday's. After all, he was a master experimenter with a lifetime of experience. The children often build devices that seem, next to his, complex and cumbersome. They sometimes go the long way around to come to the same conclusions. But there are also those times, those ecstatic moments, when they hit upon some truly ingenious demonstration that seems to transcend Faraday. Parents, educators and other children alike eagerly await those inspired reports, put together by little children working with primitive equipment, which draw tentative conclusions beyond anything Faraday could have possibly dreamed.

As we pass the current Faraday tent, we can see the outline of children's heads bending over a table. My wife and I agree to check at the Central Dome, perhaps today, to learn what the latest Faraday projects have yielded. We walk on toward the Senoi tent, where we may find Johnny.

The Senoi project is generally filled with twenty or even more children of various ages. It is a large tent with an earthen floor, recreating the bamboo, rattan and thatch environment of a primitive tribe that inhabited the central mountain range of the Malay Peninsula. Through all the wars and horrors of the eighteenth, nineteenth and twentieth centuries, this people, the Senoi, lived without a single violent crime or intercommunal conflict. They did so by employing methods of psychology and interpersonal relations that seemed, to the people of the mid-twentieth century, nothing less than astonishing. Even today, when the absence of aggression and violence doesn't seem so phenomenal, the Senoi methods make an enjoyable and effective introduction to the control of the inner impulses, of what was once called the "subconscious."

The Senoi were a hunting and fishing people, although they practiced some agriculture. But they spent a great part of each day, starting with breakfast, in dream interpretation and the follow-up activities it triggered; this was central to the education of every child. As reported by the mid-twentieth-century psychiatrist-anthropologist Kilton Stewart, a leading student of the Senoi, when a child reported a falling dream, for example, the adult would respond with enthusiasm, congratulating the child for having had one of the most powerful and useful dreams a person can have. The adult would then ask the child where he had landed after the fall and what he had learned.

The child might answer that he had been afraid and had awakened with a start. At this point, the adult would begin his instruction, explaining that every dream-act has a purpose and a destination. The dreamer must overcome his fear. He must surrender to the spirit-world and thus get in touch with its enormous powers. The adult would then ask the child to remember his words during his next falling dream and to find pleasure in traveling to the source of the power that caused him to fall.

To change the fear of falling into the joy of flying takes time and practice. But the entire Senoi social structure is set up to encourage such feats, and eventually every Senoi child learns to exchange hesitation and anxiety for curiosity and ecstasy. Every child learns to advance straight into the teeth of any dream–danger. He learns to travel all the way to any dream's destination or resolution and to bring back something that will be of use or delight to the entire tribe in its daily, waking life.

While in the tent, Kennedy children *become* Senoi. By so doing, they practice psychic mobility and gain control of their dreams, of a whole realm of thinking and feeling that was almost entirely ignored throughout the Civilized Epoch.

The great majority of Kennedy children have learned, by the age of six, to fall asleep at will. About midmorning, everyone in the Senoi tent lies down and goes through a complete sleep cycle, including at least one dream. This takes about ninety minutes. They awaken, eat and begin their dream sessions. Older children who have been Senoi children in earlier years are now Senoi adults. For the last several weeks, Johnny has been one of them, with the added responsibility of a *halak,* a psychologist-educator. He has a "wife" and two "children," a six-year-old boy and girl. When Johnny's "son" dreams that a friend has insulted him, Johnny advises him to inform his friend of this fact. The friend's "father" then tells his child that he may have offended the dreamer without really meaning to, that he may have allowed a malignant character in the dream universe to use his image in the dream. He should therefore give a present to the dreamer (Johnny's son) and go out of his way to be friendly toward him in the future. Thus, any aggression building up around the image of the friend in the dreamer's mind becomes the basis of a friendly exchange.

When the Senoi project children are not directly involved in their dream sessions, they are preparing their meals or making gifts from the type of materials available on the undeveloped Malay Peninsula or presenting the dances, poems, drum rhythms and so on they have brought back from the universe of sleep. As a *halak,* Johnny also initiates "adolescents" into the agreement trance, or cooperative reverie, that is the mark of the adult Senoi. After adolescence, if a Senoi spends a great deal of time in the trance state, he is considered a specialist in healing or in the use of extrasensory powers. Kennedy children, because of their experience in altering states of consciousness (beginning in the Basics Dome and continuing especially in the Quiet Dome and Body Dome), probably find it much easier to enter the trance than did even the Senoi themselves.

Walking on toward the Senoi tent, we pass tents where children are playing games that join what you might call math and logic with music and the sense of touch; where children are simulating the environment of space; where they are creating an even more exotic place, late nineteenth-century America. We search the Senoi display for Johnny's name. It is not there. Though we know Johnny has pretty well mastered the Senoi environment, we speculate on what other environment could have pulled him away from it.

Perhaps the playfield. We enter it through a break in the border of flowering shrubs—a large, grassy expanse of flat and rolling ground. People from earlier times might be surprised that it is unmarked by lines or artificial boundaries of any kind. The games of limitation—which include most of the sports of Civilization—faded so rapidly after the late 1980s that the last lined area disappeared from the playfield a couple of years ago. Touch football was among the last to go. In its many permutations, football was fluid and interwoven enough to remain interesting and relevant in the new age, and some Kennedy children even now play a version of it that requires no fixed boundaries and no "officials." But the aggression it sometimes encourages leaves a bad taste in the mouths of most modern children.

Baseball, by contrast, lost its relevance long ago. Played now in four major domes across the nation before small invitational audiences, baseball may be seen on some of the lesser laservision stations. Its audience, needless to say, consists mostly of men over fifty. Suffused with sweet, sleepy nostalgia, they sit near their sets late into the night, transported back to another, more complex time. Baseball, indeed, characterizes much that has passed away. Its rigid rules, its fixed angles and distances, shape players to repetitive, stereotyped behaviors. Its complete reliance on officials to enforce rules and decide close plays removes the players from all moral and personal decisions, and encourages them, in fact, to get away with whatever they can. Its preoccupation with statistics reveals its view of human worth: players are valued for how many percentage points, hits, home runs, runs batted in and the like they can accumulate. Everything is acquisitive, comparative, competitive, limiting.

Children who have played the games of expansion are hard pressed to comprehend baseball's great past appeal. As for these present games, many are improvised by the children themselves, then revised day by day. Refinement generally runs toward simplicity, elegance and an absolute minimum of rules. With no officials to intervene, the players themselves are repeatedly up against moral decisions.

On the flatland, several pairs of children are sailing plastic aerodynamic disks back and forth. We watch the disks spin, whirlpools of color in an ocean of blue sky, soaring, wheeling, slanting. One child throws. His co-player runs pell-mell to intercept the disk, diving, if necessary, to spear it one-handedly. It is a popular game, sort of an old standby. Rules may vary, but are generally quite simple: The two players stand about fifteen yards apart. When the thrower launches the disk, the receiver makes an all-out effort to reach it. If he cannot get close enough to touch the disk—i.e., if it is entirely out of his range—he takes a point. If, on the other hand, the throw turns out to have been within his range but he failed (through misjudgment or insufficient effort) to reach it, the receiver gives a point to the thrower. If the receiver manages to touch the disk and then drops it, he gives the thrower two points. In each case, the receiver makes the decision. There is no appeal, no intervening referee, no out-of-bounds sanctuary. Thus, the receiver is making frequent statements about his own ultimate capabilities. He is practicing moral judgment. The greatest joy comes from a perfectly executed throw and a spectacular catch. In this case no score whatever changes hands. The reward is intrinsic. There are no external standards, no statistical comparisons—only the absolute of individual ability, desire and honesty.

Over on the playfield's gently rolling area, we see a group of about ten children running wildly from one crest to another, then sitting in a circle. They creep catlike to the next crest, and again sit. I suggest to my wife that we stay for a while and try, as we sometimes do, to figure out that game's rationale or its essence. But she is more interested in Johnny, and we can see that he is nowhere on the field. So we head past the large Arts Dome on the edge of the playfield toward the Central Dome.

I ask my wife: "Are you hungry?"

"Yes, yes, yes."

We walk faster. Throughout the school day refreshments are served to parents and educators in the computer readout room. Comfortable chairs and lounges are arranged in informal clusters. Multiple stereo fills the room with music. One wall is lined with readout consoles, at which parents and educators alike can request data about Kennedy children. Parents, identified electronically through their EIDs, are granted information only about their own children, while educators can learn about any child in the school. (In another, smaller room, children can request and get the same kind of feedback about themselves.) In seconds, the computer will provide up-to-the-moment data on how much time a child has been spending in each of the environments. It will analyze a young child's "progress" in the Basics Dome or will show what kinds of information an older child has been requesting on his Remote Readout. It will also, upon request, provide a Uniqueness Profile or a number of other profiles, including Empathy, Joy of Learning, Body Development, Awareness, Consciousness Control and the like. Parents and children are cautioned, however, not to take these profiles very seriously. They are only rough guides to development, not evaluations in the old sense. The best thing about the computer readout room, most parents feel, is not the computer readout, but the happy atmosphere of relatedness between parents and educators—and perhaps the refreshments.

We don't quite make the Central Dome, however, in spite of our hunger. On the way, we pass a group of older children in a grassy clearing surrounded by shade trees. Something about the way they are sitting draws us nearer. We see at once that Johnny is among them and that all of them have been crying. My wife walks over slowly and rests on the grass near him. I follow. No words are spoken. We settle down and tune our consciousness to feel what these children feel. Gradually their melancholy suffuses us. I close my eyes and a wine-dark sea, sparkling with sapphire and gold, stretches to the horizons of my inner vision. I am overcome with a sense of waste, of utter loss. I open my eyes and meet those of children around me. Tears have made their eyes pale and bright. They meet my gaze directly and openly, and I feel my own tears welling up.

"We couldn't go on," Johnny says softly, handing me a history-drama script, thin pages of opaque plastic bound by spiral wire. *Thucydides: The Peloponnesian Wars.*

Nodding, I say, "I know what you mean."

"We *tried* to become Athenians. We tried to stay in character. But look . . ."

He hands me the script, pointing out a passage in "The Melian Dialogue."

> MELIAN: But must we be your enemies? Would you not receive us as friends if we are neutral and remain at peace with you?

ATHENIAN: No, your enmity does not injure us as much as your friendship; for your enmity is in the eyes of our subjects a demonstration of our power, your friendship of our weakness.

"And then," Johnny says, "the Athenians went on to massacre all the adult males in this—this little island—and made *slaves* out of all the women and children. It's hard to understand. It's hard to play the parts."

Tears start streaming down his face. "We tried to act out the Melian section yesterday afternoon, but we didn't do too well. And then this morning, we were in the Athenian Assembly making the decision to invade Sicily, and—in some ways they were such beautiful people—most of us know how it's going to come out—we all broke down and couldn't go on. We can't get anyone to play the part of Alcibiades. I don't know if we'll *ever* finish."

Overhearing Johnny's words, several children begin sobbing audibly. Two little girls crawl into my wife's arms.

"Don't worry about it, Johnny," I say. "Anyone who can relive the Peloponnesian Wars—or *any war*—without crying is somehow defective. Something's lacking."

"Yes, but isn't it true that people used to be able to read about wars without crying? *That* seems so sad. It seems kind of—crazy, or something."

"It would seem crazy to you. But I must remind you that even your grandmothers and grandfathers approached the subject that way. People studied wars with an attitude that *would* seem completely crazy. But I won't use that word; 'inhuman' is better. They were able to make the whole thing into a sort of chess game. They'd become 'experts' on something like our own Civil War of 1861, mapping campaigns with hypnotic fascination, never *feeling* anything except maybe an avid hope for one side to win or lose, or a captivation with strategy or tactics.

Sometimes they felt 'glory,' too, which isn't so much a feeling as a substitute for feeling, programmed by Civilized societies to take the place of or even block relevant personal emotions. We have to face it, Johnny, people actually could and did read about or see movies about brutal killings and senseless destruction without most of the relevant human feelings."

"But *why? How? How* did they do it?"

"*They were uneducated.* It's as simple as that. You know, Johnny, until very recently education was mostly nothing more than the 'teaching' of facts and concepts. Even as late as the 1960s, people could go completely through school and remain what might be called, in the words of those days, not only emotional imbeciles, but sensory ignoramuses and somatic dumbbells. That in itself, just as you said, is one of the saddest things of all. Crying over the absolute tragedy of war—and especially a war such as the Peloponnesian—is a part of learning, it seems to me, a way of practicing relevant emotions—a lot more important than remembering names and dates."

"But we *do* remember all those things," Johnny says. "It's hard to forget, once you've *lived* it."

"Yes, and you can live it on more than one level. With psychic mobility, you can experience what you as an Athenian of 415 B.C. feel, what you as Thucydides feel (when you're working from his text), and what you living in this age feel. And isn't there a certain common ground? Don't you sense in Thucydides an irony, an outrage, even a deep personal sorrow about the events he describes?"

"Yes, I do. We all do. It adds to the sadness."

By this time several children of the history-drama group had gathered around me and Johnny.

"Why don't you stay with us today?" one of the younger girls asks, looking first at me, then at my wife.

"Why don't you be Alcibiades?" a boy, one of Johnny's friends, asks me. "And Johnny can be Nicias, and we can start over again."

"And we'll be Athenians," the girl says with determination. "We really will."

So once again, as on so many other visits, we find ourselves drawn into one of the learning projects. This tree-circled plot becomes the Athenian Assembly. I become youthful Alcibiades with all his pride and folly, instrument of an ancient male conspiracy of "honor," "power" and "glory"; while my son is old Nicias, appointed general against his will, now counseling in vain against the madness of arrogance and empire. The hours pass. We sail to Sicily, and then down that slow, agonizing whirlpool toward annihilation; the nightmarish denouement of prideful dreams; the affirmation of Thucydides' judgment in his time that unbridled human nature, finally, is "ungovernable in passion, uncontrollable by justice and hostile to all superiors."

We emerge from the past with a new sense of communion and love. We sit silently, holding hands, in a circle. We are unashamed of our tears, unmindful of differences in age and sex. In the fading sunlight we celebrate the present. By the power of our ability to feel, we are rescued from history. We know that Thucydides was wrong; human nature is what we make it. None of this needs to be said. The moment transcends words. And I cannot tell how long it is before my wife and I, descending to another state of consciousness, remember that we have forgotten to eat.

new technology already is here (as will be seen), though no one thus far has pulled it together in a unified educational environment. In any case, lack of technological aids does not deter change. Most of the things done electronically in Kennedy School can be done *now* by human beings.

Indeed, everything in the preceding chapters is based on something that already exists. In this and the next chapter, therefore, I shall present brief descriptions of the main idea sources for Kennedy School. They represent only a small sample of the many organizations and individuals who are pressing ahead into unexplored educational territory. But they may be useful to educators, parents and students who are interested not in shoring up the present educational structure, but in building a new one. They affirm that true alternatives are possible, that a vastly expanded, efficient, joyful new education is not only possible, but imminent.

The free learner has become a favorite concept at the "free universities" scattered around the nation. But it has been hard to make the concept work in higher education. Those who have lived the academic life are prone to specialty and theory. Often, without even questioning it, they subscribe to the Academic Heresy (i.e., the "life of the mind" is all that really counts). The academic approach to free learning usually has turned out to be either negative or esoteric. Experimental colleges *remove* exams, grades and units—a good first step, perhaps. Too often, however, they fail to *add* new educational situations to take their places. And they pay too little attention to building total, involving environments. Some of the reformers in higher education have a childlike faith that, once compulsion is ended, true learning will automatically begin. It is not quite that simple.

Free universities have sometimes replaced courses in literature, history and the like with courses such as "Consciousness and Society" or "The Search for Identity"—another good move, perhaps. But these are still *courses,* with *teachers* and *students,* not real learning environments. There is great pressure for reform among the brightest college students and faculty, and a great deal of energy for experimental projects on many campuses. But the unfettered free learner may well emerge first in the lower grades.

The best free-learning school I have visited operates in a rather drab four-story building on West Fifteenth Street in New York City. The Fifteenth Street School was conceived by actor Orson Bean as a Summerhill-type institution—but with a difference. Most Summerhill offshoots are primarily negative in character; that is, they go all out to remove the coercive aspects of conventional schooling without a corresponding effort to create new motivations. The Fifteenth Street School, on the other hand, pursues basic learning passionately and successfully. It does so without compromising the principle of the free learner.

From the moment a child enters the building until he leaves, he is free to go anywhere and do anything he pleases, so long as he does not harm himself or his fellow students. Wandering through old hallways and rooms, up and down stairs, the Fifteenth Street children today exhibit the joyful intensity I imagined for children in the far more expansive environment of the twenty-first century. The building's entire ground floor is the "gym," a large rectangular space with a composition floor. In the gym, children may find various play objects—balls, bats of foam rubber, blankets, large cardboard containers. Two old upright pianos are there, and a jukebox that plays a selection of rock music for free. At the gym's far end is a low platform, and at the near end a sort of closet, in which children often create arcane little worlds that are almost impenetrable by adults.

The school's educational director, a tall, long-jawed, practical man named Wilbur Rippy, considers the gym "the most important place here. The young animal must *move*. That's what keeps him alive. All the senses are in operation here—the visual, auditory, tactile, kinesthetic. They tell the child, 'The world is really here, now.' "

It is instructive to spend a day in the gym. As children come and go, the mood of the place shifts like a summer sky. Boisterous pursuit runs its course, subsides into a time of watching and waiting. A child turns off the lights, and the only illumination filters in through windows at the far end. Now the gym is a cavern of silence and mystery. The senses become acute. Children are aware of each other— their movements, their feelings. A new group enters. Someone turns on the jukebox. Everything changes.

With the freedom to do so, why don't children spend *all* their time in the gym? The question would naturally occur to most of us, whose school experience has consisted of sitting long hours at teachers' commands, of repeating the same thing over and again, of wishing and waiting to escape. Children at Fifteenth Street leave the gym because their bodies and minds tell them they have had enough, and because other fascinating and deeply involving educational environments are available. A room where children lounge around and read, for example, is on the fourth floor, a pleasant place with chairs arranged informally at a table and cushions on the floor around the walls. A "teacher" may be there, but the child receives no instruction in the conventional sense. He uses the Sullivan programs (see Chapter II), so he can start where he left off last time. If he needs help, there are other children around to help him. Wilbur Rippy has discovered, in fact, that children make the very best teachers. Often, when a child runs up against a block in some subject such as reading, he overcomes it most easily with the help of another child rather than an adult.

There are other rooms, other environments—a woodshop, a math room, a kitchen, a quiet room, two balconies, a rooftop playground. One large room on the third floor is set aside for the arts. Every obtainable art material is made available to the children. Wilbur Rippy's wife, Rachel, remains in the room most of the time, not to instruct the children, but to help when requested and to provide feedback on what the children are doing. Another large room on the same floor contains tables, reference books and charts as well as a variety of children's books. The most striking characteristic of this room is the profusion of things that might be labeled "junk"—large wood blocks of various shapes, wires, ropes, all sorts of surplus electronic equipment and other machinery. Here, children can create their own worlds, their own learning environments.

During the time of my visits, a six-and-a-half-year-old named Alan had invented a learning environment for himself so efficient, involving and complete that educators at all levels might well learn from it. Since Alan's basic metaphor was war, I was at first somewhat put off. Then I realized that he, more than anyone I had met, hated and feared war and the consciousness of war that pervades American life. It was as if, by understanding war down to the roots, he might gain some sort of dominion over it.

Alan's home base was a corner of the reading-reference-junk room. There he had built an impressive fortress that changed in character and armaments as the campaign he was imagining changed. Alan spent quite a bit of time, helmeted and armed, within the fortress. But he spent far more time at what he called "my work." His work consisted of filling large sketch pads with line drawings of battle situations. Vivid and accurate in detail, the drawings were produced with great speed and economy of line. When I told him my own combat experience had, fortunately, kept me out of trenches, he said, "Do you want to see what trench warfare is like?" and leafed through a completed sketch pad. The sketch he showed gave me the *experience* of being in a World War I trench—the cramped surroundings, tangles of barbed wire, exploding shells, the distant yet ominous presence of the enemy.

After a couple of days, I learned that Alan's "work" involved a project of grand proportions: he was creating a picture history of every major war the U.S. had fought, from the Revolutionary War through Vietnam. At the time of my visit, he was up to the North African Campaigns of World War II. When Alan needed further information about some battle or mode of warfare, he would take a book about the campaign (generally written at the eleven- or twelve-year-old level), retire to a corner and read avidly. No "motivation" problem here. Or he would go to the art room and paint combatants' flags and insignias, or model tanks and warships in clay. In the woodshop, Alan would build appropriate armaments. In the gym, he would invent war games. Or, in a perfectly reasonable switch, he would organize peace marches, with hand-lettered signs ("War is sick").

Perhaps not by accident, Alan's headquarters were located within easy hearing distance of the table where Wilbur Rippy read aloud about and discussed history, geography, evolution, etc. While Rippy would read, Alan would continue his work, hardly seeming to notice the "lesson," but actually taking it all in. When Rippy would leave, Alan would rush to the table, scan the written material, look at the pictures, study the specimens, then mutter: "I must get back to my work."

Reading, of course, was no problem for Alan. He didn't have to waste his time, as he would in the usual school, sitting listening to others labor over words. As for math, I asked an evaluation from the youngish woman who generally handles that environment. "Alan drops by about once or twice a week," she told me. "He works the problems and then verbalizes the concept as well as anyone there. After five or ten minutes, he says, 'I must get back to my work,' and he's off."

Children at Fifteenth Street bring their own lunches and they can eat whenever they wish. (Some eat as soon as they arrive.) On one of the days of my visit, Alan's mother, upon picking him up at the end of school, was heard to exclaim: "Oh, no. You haven't forgotten to eat your lunch *again!*" That a child can become so involved with his "work" that he forgets to eat is only one measure of how ecstatic education can be.

I do not like to think what would happen to a child like Alan in a conventional school. Forget the psychological pain, the human tragedy for a moment if you can, and consider just the inefficiency—and not only for a child like Alan, but for all children. If human beings are individual and unique, then any system of fixed scheduling and mass instruction must be insanely inefficient. It may *seem* tidy and convenient, but that is an illusion maintained only by pretending that individual differences are not significant and that the human potential is incredibly low—only by giving up on education and concentrating on control. For an educator of courage and flexibility, the free-learning situation is not only more educationally efficient but, eventually, easier to handle. Best start with the youngest. Children who have been sat upon for years in conventional classrooms might simply explode for a while when first placed in the free-learning situation. Experience with transfers to Fifteenth Street School, however, has shown that children quickly adapt. To the uninitiated observer, the free-learning situation may sometimes seem noisy and confused on the surface. The conventional classroom may seem quiet and orderly on the surface. The noise and confusion there are in the minds of the children.

Fifteenth Street School has neither computer nor Electronic Identification Devices to keep track of how long each child spends in each environment. The educators perform this function. They make it their business to know (if not with mathematical precision) where and how each child spends his time. If a child stays in the gym *all* the time, for example, the educators try to figure out why, then set up learning situations for him that will draw him out. Since the school is still small (sixty children, five educators) the children are easily tracked. (Larger schools may be broken down into equally small units.) If nothing more, Fifteenth Street School shows that free learning in the early grades is possible and certainly not incompatible with the rather unambitious, narrow "academic" goals that constitute present-day education.

The total environment has been a central theme throughout this exploration of education and ecstasy. No act of learning exists in a vacuum. It is only when the learning environment is viewed and acted upon as a whole that education can become truly efficient and joyful. Most schools do not run twenty-four hours a day. But the inspired and devoted participation of parents can help link the broken days together. The best innovative schools tend to draw parents closely into the circle of learning.

The total environment, the interrelatedness of everything within an educational setting, should quickly become apparent to those within large corporations who are now analyzing education in terms of systems engineering. Thus far, the systems people have tended to dial into their systems only those aspects of education which currently are considered the schools' domain—which is to say, very little, indeed. However, if the new educational engineers keep their feedback circuits open, that is, if they truly keep learning from what they are analyzing, I feel it inevitable that their concern will widen.

The question remains, Can a total, controlled environment really change human behavior, deep down? If proof is needed, an organization called Synanon offers proof positive. Not the most deep-rooted character disorders or the most "hopeless" forms of drug addiction or even "human nature" itself have proven immune to its powerful, twenty-four-hour-a-day educational techniques. And education is precisely what Synanon's leaders conceive their work to be.

It is difficult to treat this organization at less than book length. (*The Tunnel Back* by Dr. Lewis Yablonsky is probably the best written on the subject.) Upon first examination, Synanon seems rife with contradictions. When you try to compare it to a better-known organization, the comparison inevitably leaves something lacking. Its structure is hierarchical, even paramilitary; and yet it pursues the highest human freedoms. In one of its educational settings (the Synanon Game), a lowly new member may be praised for screaming insults at the director; in another setting, he might be asked to have his head shaved if he muttered far less to his immediate boss. Its theorists follow the concepts of Maslow (peak experience, self-actualization) and Rogers (humanist values, noncondi-tional love), while feeling some of the usual humanist distaste for the radical behaviorism of Skinner; and yet, a Synanon house is blatantly Skinnerian, with "reinforce-ment" a favorite operational term. None of this is really contradictory.

Synanon was founded in 1958 by Charles (Chuck) Ded-erich as a way of dealing with drug addiction. Dederich got an old house on the beach at Santa Monica, California, and set up a tightly structured living situation in which the addict had to face the direct short-term and long-term consequences of his every act. The value system on which he based the Synanon reinforcement system was, in gen-eral, the one preached (but not lived) by the outside soci-ety—absolute honesty, personal responsibility, cooperation, love. History gave Dederich little chance of success: every therapy since Freud had been all but helpless against the character problems tied up with addiction. Dederich, how-ever, offered not therapy and theories, but close attention to living, i.e., *education* in a total environment, designed to *change* people. What happened? Of all addicts who have to come to Synanon, more than half are still "clean."

But that, for Dederich and his lieutenants, is only a be-ginning. At this writing, Synanon operates houses in Santa Monica, San Francisco, San Diego and Marshall, Califor-nia, New York City and Detroit. It runs an advertising-specialties business and several service stations.

Around 1,000 men, women and children live full time in Synanon houses. In addition, some 2,500 "squares" (nonaddicts) are members of the Synanon Game Club, which means they spend several hours at least one night a week at a Synanon facility. Though Synanon first set up its education for people in the dire straits of addiction, its ultimate aim is nothing less than the creation of a giant, utopian "communiversity" with millions of members representing every walk of life. This communiversity would influence the society at large through its example of rectitude and realization, and perhaps through economic and political pressure.

Addicts come to Synanon voluntarily, "through the front door." A newcomer must abide by two absolute prohibitions: no drugs, including alcohol, and no violence. He also agrees to give up all his material possessions to the organization and not to communicate with any of his friends or relatives for ninety days. Thus he is effectively removed from the old environment, the set of reinforcements that caused him to become addicted in the first place.

Deprived of narcotics, the newcomer begins his physical withdrawal from addiction. He does so on a couch in the living room of the house, in full view of all who pass. He is not reinforced by undue pity and attention for such behavior as writhing on the floor. To the contrary. In these circumstances, the process turns out to be far less histrionic than usually portrayed in the cinema. A moment comes when the withdrawal symptoms have gone. The newcomer looks up expectantly: "I've kicked it!" He smiles for congratulations. He is the prodigal son. Where is his feast of praise? Someone hands him a mop.

The members of Synanon know that old pattern too well. The addict will get himself a habit just so he can kick it and become the prodigal son to his mother, his girl friend, his buddies, in an endless cycle. Synanon members are too Skinnerian to reinforce an organism for something they don't want it to do again. The newcomer will get his reinforcement for doing his job (initially a lowly job) and for becoming a responsible member of a responsive community. He will not be reinforced for gaining "insight" into his "problems" or for analyzing his "sickness." For Synanon, people with character disorders are not "sick" or "bad." They are simply stupid. They are *uneducated*—perhaps not verbally or conceptually, but morally and emotionally. Their education consists of facing the consequences of their acts, moment by moment, day by day, in an environment so total that no escape into stupidity is possible. Traditional psychiatry is turned on its head. Rather than verbally probing the unconscious so they can understand their unhealthy urges, *then* do something about them, Synanon members face situations where they must go ahead and change their *actions*. When they do this, their feelings about themselves and others change. Insights may follow, but are considered simply explanatory of why the person is *already* acting and feeling differently.

The Synanon Game, played by ex-addicts and "squares" alike, stands somewhat at the other end of the behavior spectrum. Groups of from eight to twelve sit in chairs in a circle and express themselves with all the vehemence they can muster. There are no prohibitions here except against physical violence or offers of it. As in basic encounter groups, absolute honesty is sought, and a premium is placed upon present feelings. A greater than usual stress, however, is put upon aggression and attack. Synanon leaders describe the Game as "a verbal street fight." In the Game setting, a person finds he can express forbidden feelings openly and honestly, without fear of reprisals. He can also hear the worst about himself without collapsing in self-pity or turning to drugs or other escapes offered by the society at large. Each participant gets the kind of feedback about his own behaviors that is simply not available outside. And he receives it in direct, active encounter, involving his own responses. Thus he learns, he changes. Synanon residents play the Game at least three nights a week; nonresident "squares" generally play weekly.

Synanon has devised several other educational techniques: regular noon seminars for all residents; daylong or weeklong "Cerebrations," during which members interact and become deeply involved on matters that tend toward the intellectual; "Dissipations," during which select members (not newcomers) engage in marathon encounter sessions lasting up to thirty hours at a stretch, and during which, in the words of a Synanon leader, "peak experiences by the bushel are guaranteed—visions, mystical experiences, whatever."

Here, then, is a determined, ornery, proselytizing outfit that started out solving a previously insoluble human problem and that is now on the way toward an almost mystical "trip." Chuck Dederich says that "straightening out people whose head is screwed on sideways is only a side effect." But the fact remains that Synanon has been shaped by the kind of people it first dealt with. These people were so damaged (or "addicted to stupidity," in Dederich's words) by the outside environment that they required tight reins in the new environment. Rigid, authoritarian structure *works* for them, but probably needs to be modified as Synanon expands into the larger community.

Nonetheless, by tackling the impossible first, Synanon has affirmed, beyond any doubt, the power of a changed environment to change (educate) human beings.

Technological aids to education are not hard to imagine for the future because there are so many around right now. In fact, with all those large corporations presently planning school computers and other hardware, educators already are hard pressed to pick the wheat from the chaff.

The magnitude of our technological effort makes possible errors of great magnitude. For example, one teacher lecturing to thirty or 300 students with minimal feedback is inefficient enough. But it took the ingenuity and grandeur of American technology to make it possible (on "educational" TV) for one teacher to lecture simultaneously to hundreds of thousands of students with no feedback whatever. The results of this kind of TV teaching have been discouraging even to its backers.

The free learner in a total school environment will tend to serve as a check against error in selecting hardware. If an educational environment does not work in this setting, the educator finds out about it soon enough. Not so with students chained to their desks by day, overloaded with homework by night and forced to take exams against their will. Hardware might also be judged as to how it enhances the learner's pleasure. Even on narrow, practical grounds, joy of learning will generally prove to increase efficiency of learning. Beyond efficiency, technological aids to education might be judged as to how well they fulfill the new educational goals. Whether these goals resemble those suggested in Chapter VII or not, they will probably depart, sooner than we think, from the tacit, limiting goals of today.

In any case, the technology is on its way, and we can make what we will of it. The Basics Dome in Kennedy School is simply a projection of present reality. For several years, Dr. Omar Khayam Moore has been using various versions of a "talking typewriter" to teach children as young as three to read, write, spell and compose little stories. Dr. Moore now carries on his work at the Learning Research and Development Center of the University of Pittsburgh. This brief description of his project is taken from *The Computer in American Education,* edited by Don D. Bushnell and Dwight W. Allen in 1967:

The Edison Responsive Environment Instrument (ERE) is a computerized typewriter with capabilities intended to reproduce several of the response actions of a human teacher. When a pupil depresses a key on the typewriter keyboard, the key symbol is typed in large type on the typewriter paper and is pronounced at the same time. On a rear projection screen, letters, words, and sentences can be displayed automatically with accompanying audio explanations and pointer designations. The keyboard can be locked except for the key the child is expected to press. As well as playing the model soundtrack, the device can record and play back the child's voice for comparison purposes.

Typically, the instrument is programmed to point out a particular letter, play the recording of the pronunciation, and free only the correct key to be pressed by the student. The program proceeds to the next letter or word or sentence after the correct key has been pressed.

Dr. Patrick Suppes of the Institute for Mathematical Studies in the Social Sciences at Stanford University is among the other researchers who are using the computer and the learning console to increase the ease and efficiency of conventional education. At the Brentwood Elementary School in East Palo Alto, California, students learn language and math skills from electronic tutors. Suppes' young learners communicate with the computer not only through a keyboard, but by using a "light pen" to touch right answers on the display.

At the college level, the Penn State Multi-Media Building and the PLATO (Programmed Logic for Automatic Teaching Operations) project at the University of Illinois exemplify the academic approach to electronic education.

All these projects, in comparison to what they can become, must be looked upon as crude and rudimentary. They lack, most of all, a sense of fun, of play, of sheer delight. Their developers may be too enthralled with the hardware itself to view that rare if quite urgent vision of learning as ecstatic, as an art form.

Such a vision is realized in some of the most powerful learning environments I have visited, the light-and-sound ballrooms that were first developed in San Francisco in 1965. Like Kennedy's Basics Dome, the Fillmore Auditorium and the Avalon Ballroom overwhelm the senses at first impact. Two walls overflow with swirling, everchanging visual images. Motion pictures appear briefly, to reappear a hundred feet away on another wall. Still pictures flash on, only to be transformed into something ingeniously unrelated; a rock band becomes a scene of medieval falconry. Images race from one end of the panorama to the other, while liquid colors flow in slow eddies. At one end of the ballroom, powerful ultraviolet lamps pour out black light; beneath these lamps, hair, eyes, teeth, clothing suddenly are *different*. So, we learn, the sternest, safest colors are by no means fixed and permanent. Appearance can be changed in a twinkling. Under the black light, impromptu artists with luminescent paint cover the floor with glowing tapestries or paint each others' faces, hands, boots. Transfiguration now. From a side wall, a jarring strobe light flashes. Slowly at first, then quickening with the intensity of the music and the dancing, the flashes approach ten cycles a second, the approximate rate of the ongoing alpha wave in the brain. Some dancers surrender their brain-wave tempo to the light (in brain research, this process is termed "brain driving") and enter another realm; everything about them seems to float and they themselves, dreamlike, glide above a floor that no longer seems necessarily level and fixed.

Some practitioners of this new art/education form, the light-and-sound show, have found a way to connect lights to the sound amplifier so that the intensity, frequency and hue of the show reflect the intensity, tempo and pitch of the music. I have also heard (but have not been able to run down) a rumor that experimenters in the Los Angeles area have used human brain waves through an EEG to influence a light show. There is no technical reason that this cannot be done quite easily.

Indeed, the chief learning derived from these marvelous environments is on the nature of the possible. This learning is sensory, somatic and conceptual, if you will. But there is also more specific learning: When my daughter Lillie started first grade, she was a fine artist. That is to say, she produced drawings and paintings that delighted me, my wife and our friends; she produced them in great quantity; she was happy and deeply involved while producing them. After six months of art instruction (in a conventional classroom, alas), her voluntary art production had dropped almost to zero. The art she did produce was tight, stereotyped and completely uninspired. She wondered if the cow she drew would match the cow of the stencil (yes, really) her teacher had given her. She worried about being neat, about coloring within the lines.

One Sunday afternoon, I took her to the Fillmore Auditorium. It was crowded; she sat on my shoulders and I eased up to the middle of the dance floor. Ten or fifteen minutes passed before she spoke, and then it was one word, uttered during a break in the music with such awe and conviction that I can still hear it: *"Wow!"*

When we got home, Lillie sat down and began drawing with an entirely new sweep and freedom that showed a definite Fillmore influence. In the months that have followed (we returned another afternoon with some luminescent paint to use beneath the black light), Lillie's art output has been prodigious. She has produced drawings, paintings, colored masks, clay models, collages and some objects that defy categorization. Rarely is a single learning experience so powerful and long-lasting. But the Fillmore was not designed by pedants to *teach* in a dutiful, limiting, linear fashion. It was designed by a new kind of artist to produce ecstasy. And an ecstatic environment, providing appropriate materials as in Kennedy's Basics Dome, can produce a learning rate fantastic by all present standards.

There is no technical reason that something very similar to the Basics Dome could not be set up right now. The computerized learning displays could be arranged around the inner wall of a circular building. The visual materials to be used on the displays would be conceived and created with far more verve, humor and artistry than is now the case. A skilled light-show team, working from an elevated platform in the center of the building, could produce a constant, 360-degree light show. Observing the learners' progress and the nature of their learning material, they could provide much of the novelty, excitement and sense of community provided by Cross-Matrix Stimulus and Response and Communal Interconnect in Kennedy School.

Visionary? It may seem so to those who persist in omitting the Dionysian factor from the educational equation, who are willing to tolerate countless physical and psychic dropouts, who can bear for our schools to limp along in their present agony. No, I am not suggesting *specifically* that we immediately combine the work of men like Moore and Suppes with the work of the hip innovators to create a sort of do-it-yourself Basics Dome. But I am saying that we *can*. I am expanding, if only modestly, the realm of the possible. I am holding up a vision to encourage visions in others. In these times, nothing less is even respectable.

spected institutions have begun to show strong interest in helping education break out of the old subject-matter entrapment. A Ford Foundation official has become an authority on what he calls "affective education" (as opposed to "cognitive education"). The prestigious Twentieth Century Fund held a series of "Human Potential Luncheons" during 1966 and 1967 in New York City. Speakers at these luncheons ranged far beyond the conventional boundaries of education and psychology, even as far as speculation on extrasensory perception. (My own presentation, "Towards Basic Changes in Education," summarized some of the ideas in this book.) The Bureau of Research of the increasingly powerful and innovative U. S. Office of Education is becoming deeply involved in exploring the new domain. For its future studies, the Bureau has called upon (among other innovative organizations) the Western Behavioral Sciences Institute and Stanford Research Institute to probe into possibilities that lie beyond the present scope of schooling.

The one place you would go to find most of the new domain drawn together in some sort of coherent whole is an unlikely institute that psychologist Abraham Maslow has called "probably the most important educational institute in the world." To get there, you would drive south from Monterey, California, forty-five miles along the edge of the Pacific on one of the more spectacular roads in this hemisphere. Of this Coast Road, that at some places soars over a thousand feet above the sea, poet Robinson Jeffers wrote: "Beautiful beyond belief/ The heights glimmer in the sliding cloud, the great bronze gorge-cut sides of the mountain tower up invincibly/ Not the least hurt by this ribbon of road carved on their sea-foot."

The road would lead you to a cluster of cabins, a small dome, a rustic lodge, some meeting rooms, a swimming pool and hot mineral baths—all thrusting seaward on a point of land above the Pacific. This site was the home, up into the nineteenth century, of a tribe of Indians who called themselves the "Esalen." They fished in the ocean and the cold stream that cascades down an adjoining red-wood canyon, hunted small game in the canyon, foraged for acorns and roots in fertile soil and worshiped the medicinal powers of the hot springs that gush from the hills all around. It is from this Indian tribe, not an acronym, that Esalen Institute takes its name.

Just as Synanon reflects the crusty personality of its founder, Chuck Dederich, Esalen reflects Michael Murphy, its youthful president and co-founder (with fellow-seeker Richard Price). In a thirties-type movie, Murphy would be type-cast as the student-body president (which he was, at Salinas, California, High). In a Western, he would be the Good Guy, too good-looking, too gentle and thoughtful for his own good, but capable of that final, necessary resolve.

Esalen's open-mindedness and inspired eclecticism (reflecting Murphy) are probably what accounts for its having become, since its modest beginnings in 1961, the freest marketplace for new ideas in the behavioral sciences of our time. I cannot claim objectivity (if such exists) on this subject. It is only fair to say that Michael Murphy is a close friend and that I have served as vice-president of the institute since 1966. Objective or not, I am unable to imagine an institute other than Esalen where people have enjoyed free-swinging weekends with such experts as Arnold Toynbee, Linus Pauling, the late Paul Tillich, Carl Rogers, B. F. Skinner, Frederick Perls, Joseph Campbell, Abraham Maslow, Alan Watts, Buckminster Fuller and others of their caliber—interspersed with seminars or workshops presided over by lesser-known but perhaps even more innovative leaders, meetings with such titles as "Sensory Awakening for Couples," "The Self and Physical Movement," "Meditation," and "A Workshop in Bio-Energetic Analysis." It is certainly the only place in the world where you would find arch-behaviorist Skinner delightedly giving a weekend "On Programming Nonverbal Behavior," or where a supercerebral seminar by British critic Colin Wilson would be immediately followed by a weeklong workshop on "Meditative Techniques and Depth Imagery."

When, in 1961, Aldous Huxley called for a great new effort in what he termed "the nonverbal humanities," he was able to cite only a handful of examples of what he was talking about. More than 650 Esalen seminars and workshops since then have revealed that the new domain is teeming with activity. In fact, every new area of education imagined for Kennedy School (with one exception) has been explored to some extent at Esalen Institute. A residential program was initiated in September 1966, in which graduate-level fellows spend nine months as full-time free learners in the new domain. They practice meditation, intensified inner imagery, basic encounter, sensory awareness, expressive physical movement and creative symbolic behavior. They learn to control their brain-wave patterns, using the simple brain-wave feedback device developed by Dr. Joe Kamiya of University of California Medical Center. They do extensive dream work, with the Senoi methods described in our school of the future. They also practice the all-action, antianalytical Gestalt Therapy developed by the venerable Frederick Perls, in residence at the Institute.

Even the Faraday project at Kennedy School was inspired by the work of a man I met at an Esalen Seminar, Dr. J. Richard Suchman. Suchman, then an official in the

U.S. Office of Education, founded Inquiry Development, an educational approach that helps children work out their own concepts of the way the world is. Inquiring for themselves, fifth and sixth graders, for example, have come up with explanations of Archimedes' Principle that Dr. Suchman considers in some ways more elegant and precise than Archimedes'. Suchman is now developing Inquiry materials for large-scale distribution. In my view, the only weakness in the approach is that it was developed for the now existing classroom-and-teacher situation. The Kennedy Faraday project simply takes the Inquiry approach to its inevitable, child-and-environment, free-learning conclusion.

Like Synanon, Esalen resists description at less than book length. Any single episode, out of context, may make it *harder* to understand. Two visitors may report quite accurately on their particular experiences and discover little in common. Since so much of Esalen is truly experimental, nothing can be guaranteed to "work." Yet, most people who participate come away with the conviction that they have somehow been changed. And many of the Esalen experiments resonate with a characteristic sense of hope and an assumption that even the most intractable human problems contain within them the seeds of their own solution.

One such experiment took place on a July weekend in 1967, at a time when race riots were troubling many of the nation's cities. The experiment had been announced in the Esalen brochure under the rather unfortunate title "Racial Confrontation as Transcendental Experience." The brochure went on in the same vein:

> Racial segregation exists among people with divided selves. A person who is alien to some part of himself is invariably separated from anyone who represents that

alien part. The historic effort to integrate black man and white has involved us all in a vast working out of our divided human nature. Racial confrontation can be an example for all kinds of human encounter. When it goes deep enough—past superficial niceties and role-playing—it can be a vehicle for transcendental experience. Price Cobbs, a Negro psychiatrist from San Francisco, and George Leonard, a white journalist and author born and raised in Georgia, will conduct a marathon group encounter between races. The group will try to get past the roles and attitudes that divide its participants, so that they may encounter at a level beyond race.

Price Cobbs and I had okayed that brave overstatement some months before the event was to occur. On the Friday night the confrontation began both of us were feeling qualms. Here they were, thirty-five people of mixed race who had driven for miles over tricky roads to "work out their divided human natures." Could we help them past "superficial niceties and role-playing"? Could we deliver "transcendence" in a weekend?

The question gained urgency from the fast-worsening situation in the cities. It was the weekend of the Newark Black Power conference, and Price had been asked to go as a speaker. Only with considerable guilt had he begged off in favor of the improbable experiment at Big Sur.

We had planned the experiment out of a growing need, almost a desperation, for *some*thing that could show a way, even if a small one, through the racial impasse that had almost brought the civil-rights movement to a halt. The traditional ways weren't working. The Black Power militants screamed their hurt, anger and hatred. By revealing themselves and voicing the truth, they begged for encounter. The white leaders responded with conventional language, revealing nothing of their own feelings. How could there be understanding without self-revelation? Didn't the whites feel outrage, fear, repressed prejudice? The measured, judicious response seemed to us a lie. Nor was there real encounter in the biracial committees set up in some cities. Blacks and whites sat around tables, mouthed slogans, established "positions" and made "decisions" of an intellectual and political nature. They generally left the meetings unchanged. Little education took place. What would happen when we ventured into the dangerous territory where nothing is hidden?

We sat in a circle in a rustic meeting room, warmed against the cool sea air by candlelight and an open fire. Price and I outlined tentative plans for the weekend, after which each person around the circle introduced himself and offered reasons for attending—awkward, neatly wrapped statements that would be utterly shattered before the weekend was through. We started the confrontation with a technique borrowed from Dr. William Schutz. In this "Microlab," participants would have a chance to practice several ways of revealing and communicating feelings in the shortest possible time.

We asked people to take their chairs and form four separate circles of about eight each. I invited them to go along with a series of simple exercises in human relations. I suggested they start with the assumption that, within the hour, they would be relating on levels generally unknown in the community at large. Throughout the exercises, they would follow the familiar encounter rules: (1) Be completely honest and open. Forget about conventional politeness and reserve. Express anything you wish, no matter how shocking it may seem. (2) Relate on the level of feelings. Don't theorize or rationalize. (3) Stay in the here and now. Don't escape into past events or future plans. Only one prohibition: No physical violence, please.

In the first exercise, the groups would try this on their own for about ten minutes. Soon the room was alive with the kind of chatter you hear at cocktail parties. Price and I moved from circle to circle, listening in. After about seven minutes, we stopped them and offered our reactions. We had heard a lot of polite laughter. Expressions of negative feelings had been accompanied by humor that might soften the impact and take the heat off the speaker. Not that we had anything against humor, but it could so easily serve to avoid the kind of confrontation we were hoping for this weekend. Charm, too, could be a cop-out; several people were practicing it quite skillfully. The group by the door had somehow slid into the past tense, talking about former experiences and attitudes toward race, dodging the dangers and rewards of the present. As for the group nearest the fire, it was hopelessly tangled in the abstract. Members were vying with one another to spin theories that would "explain" just why they were there and how they felt. The realm of ideas is powerful, fascinating and always to be valued. But at this moment it wouldn't help us attain our goal. We asked the groups to try once more.

Now there was a change in tone. The room became quieter, more somber. We sensed premonitions of the tensions that might erupt. Tentatively, hesitantly, people began revealing themselves. But they softened each "insult" with a self-deprecatory grimace; they smiled gently at what might bring tears. And the group near the fire was back at its intellectualizing again.

After about ten minutes, we stopped the groups. Several people protested that they were just getting started. Price and I considered this an encouraging sign. We went on to the next exercise. The groups would stand in circles. Each person, in turn, would go around confronting each other person in the circle. He would look him in the eyes, touch him in some honest way (a handshake, an embrace, a finger in the chest, whatever), and tell him what he felt about him at that moment. This one-to-one situation encouraged a more direct and honest dialogue. Theorizing became more difficult. And the participants were introduced to the use of physical touch as a medium of communication.

Price and I sensed a new intentness in the room, but again we stopped the exercise before its completion. More vehement sounds of protest. We asked the groups if they would sit and try communicating for ten minutes without the use of words. They could touch, move, hum, dance—anything but talk. And they could practice a skill generally forgotten or forbidden by our culture: they could look directly and openly at another person for an extended period without having to justify it. This kind of engaged silence has a particular potency. Several people later told us it was only here they really began to feel something happening.

Ten minutes passed. We were reluctant to intervene. Most people in the circles had joined hands; though some, true to their feelings, had refused. Fifteen minutes. Complete dialogues transpired without words. People learned. Finally, Price broke the silence.

In the last exercise, the circles stood again and were asked to move slowly closer together. Inevitably, most people ended up tightly linked, arms around each other's shoulders. An artificial, manipulated integration? Perhaps. Nevertheless, people experienced a kind of closeness with strangers of various races they might previously have considered only in the abstract.

We asked the groups to sit again and try what they had tried at the beginning. Use words, sounds, touch, movement, silence—anything that would express true, here-and-now feelings. The difference was startling. It was by no means a deep confrontation, but it was a beginning. Entirely departed was the cocktail-party chatter. A few barriers had been crossed and a few eyes were moist with the wonder or relief that often accompanies such crossings. Price and I let the groups go without further interference. Gradually, the participants drifted out, most of them down the steep seaside path that leads to the hot mineral baths. The bathhouse juts out on a cliff high above a rocky beach. It is open to starlight, moonlight, the sound of surf, the chill ocean air. Up to my neck in the steaming water with members of the group, I felt comforted and mellow. Here were people of good will who were willing to be close. How could they harbor calamitous hostilities?

The next morning I began to find out. Contrary to usual practice, we held the whole group together rather than breaking it into two. This was mainly Price's idea. He wanted to keep the two of us in the same encounter. The example of our relationship, he felt, might prove useful, especially if the group ran into a complete impasse.

The first confrontations started, however, not between black and white, but among the blacks. The morning was shattered by their bitter accusations. "Racist," "Uncle Tom," and "fink" were among the milder words that went slashing back and forth across the room. "When they come with machine guns and barbed wire," one Negro said, "all I want to know is, baby, are you for me or against me?" By lunchtime, the atmosphere was electric. But there had been more accusation than true encounter. No one had really changed very much. There had been little education.

After lunch, the marathon began. We would stay in uninterrupted session through the night. Dinner would be brought to us. We would keep at it until the conventional defenses against feeling were broken down, even if it took until noon the next day. It didn't take nearly that long.

We had planned to begin the marathon with a period of sensory awakening, led by Bernard Gunther, an innovator in the field. Gunther would take us through exercises designed to make us aware of a bit of the rich sensory universe this culture commonly denies us. Because of the multi-racial nature of the group, he planned to have us keep our eyes closed during the entire session. Prejudice, he felt, is visual. When we touched an unseen stranger, we would have to deal with him in a way that would bypass racial stereotypes. But a hitch developed. Many people were anxious to get on with the encounter. Only about half the group went out on the sunlit terrace to do the exercises. I accompanied them. Price stayed with the ones inside.

It was a bizarre experience for me. As I went through Gunther's exercises, I could hear the voices but not the words from the meeting room. Eyes closed, we groped our way around the terrace and found a partner. Touching hands, we "got acquainted," had a "quarrel," "made up," tried to express love or liking, and so on. At the same time, the counterpoint from inside rose: excitement, anger, pleading and finally a burst of loud sobbing and wailing. I knew the encounter was finally under way. (Who could deeply and truly experience the reality of racial prejudice without crying?) Sweat ran down my chest and sides. I wanted to continue the Gunther experiment and at the same time be inside. At last the outside group ended with a long, unrestrained shout. Those inside found this counter-point equally bizarre.

We crowded back into the meeting room to find that everything had changed. The dialogue was on an unfa-miliar level. The faces looked unashamedly tragic and yet strangely radiant. We seemed to come from a different world. We were an intrusion, yet grudgingly accepted as the encounter rushed on.

What had caused the breakthrough, I later learned, was this: A young Japanese-American named Larry had driven up from Los Angeles with his friend, a personable light-skinned Negro named Cliff. Both of them were college students in business administration. They were making it in the white world and had tried to numb themselves to racial hurt. They were cool and cynical. They wore their masks well. But all the vehement racial talk, and especially the attacks among the blacks, had turned something upside down in them. Larry had begun talking. He had not realized how deeply he had felt racial prejudice or how much it had ruled his life. But now he knew he was a yellow man, a "Jap," and was ready to admit it. He declared himself to be a soul brother. With this declaration, all of his reserve collapsed and he "burst" into tears. The dikes were down then, and several of the Negroes poured out their hurt. "How many of you people can realize," a mother asked, "what it's like to send your children off to school and know they'll probably be called 'nigger' or spat on? And there's nothing, *nothing* you can do about it?"

When the outside group came in, Larry's friend, Cliff, was locked in a bitter encounter with a beautiful young white schoolteacher named Pam. She had told him she wanted his friendship, and he had responded scathingly, denouncing her "pitiful, condescending" overtures. Now her eyes were filled with tears.

"*Please.* What can I do? I'm trying. Please help me."

Cliff rocked his chair back and forth, looking across the room at her with contempt.

"No, baby, I'm not going to help you. I'm not going to take you off the hook. I want you to feel just what I feel.

I want you to feel what I've felt for twenty-one years. Go on. Cry."

"Please," she begged. Tears streamed down her cheeks.

Cliff kept rocking back and forth, his eyes fixed on hers. No one came to her aid. Somehow it seemed right that this interval in time should be fully realized by everyone in the room. The silence intensified, became in itself a powerful medium of communication. We began to *know* each other. At last, the silence seemed to unfold and we were talking again, the exchanges crackling around the room faster than the rational mind could follow.

Though any number of "subjects" came up in the hours that followed, the main theme through dinner and for some time thereafter was the Negroes' hurt and anger and despair, their absolute distrust of all whites. (Several times Price said that he did trust me. This had the effect of taking me off the hook, something always wished for in the hot and heavy of an encounter, but regretted afterwards.) At one point I suggested that whites, too, have their problems, their tragedies. But this was not accepted. A Negro mother said, "I just can't buy that. Whatever's wrong with you, you can do something about. But I can't do *anything* about the color of my skin—or my children's. Compared to us, you've got it made."

After darkness fell, we split the group in two for the night. Price took his half to a meeting room in another building. Without him, I felt forlorn in the vortex of all the anger and hate. But it was something we had to get through. There was no way *around* it if we wanted to accomplish our goal. By ten o'clock every white in my group was in utter despair. "I had no *idea* it was this bad," a middle-aged white woman said. "I work with Negroes. That's my *job*. And I didn't realize. My best friend of fifteen years is a Negro, and I had no idea she felt these kind of things, and now I know she does and has just been keeping them from me to spare me. I don't want to go back home. I'm afraid to see my friend. I don't see how the race problem can *ever* be solved." I told her I was glad it was all coming out in the open. The race problem could certainly never be solved so long as we *didn't* know and feel and experience the truth.

About this time, an episode began that was to occupy us, off and on, for most of the night. We had let a newcomer join the group at dinnertime. Chuck was in his early twenties, almost jet black, with a wary face and a body as taut as a steel spring. He began telling the group how he had successfully "transcended" the entire matter of race. He was utterly lacking in bad feelings against whites. He disliked the system, but not the man. He thought that racial incidents were extremely rare, especially in his own life. He never felt anger or hostility.

No one believed him. "It makes me nervous just to hear your voice," I told him. "That singsong way you have of talking, like there's no relation between what you're saying and what you feel. It puts me on edge. I feel like yelling at you." Someone suggested that I do so, and I did. Others followed me, cursing, yelling and cajoling as they expressed their feelings toward him and his professed attitude. But nothing moved Chuck. His face became a mask of stone. He had nothing but love for all mankind, the stone said. The group united in trying to get through to him. Black and white worked together. Cliff and Pam, the afternoon's bitterness forgotten, operated like a team. There was an unspoken accord among the eighteen people in the group that somehow, no matter how long it took, we would get through to Chuck. It was grinding, exhausting work, as if we were trying to penetrate a huge granite boulder with a hand drill.

At about 2:30 A.M. there came a moment of relief. A tall engineer with a thin moustache, excoriated earlier as the last of the old-time white liberals, began boasting about how many social contacts he had with Negroes. Then, with a slight smile of self-revelation, he said: "Actually, I collect Negroes." Perhaps it was not that the remark struck us as funny, but that we all needed so desperately to laugh. In any case, we exploded. "Do you have a good connection?" someone managed to gasp. "Oh, yes, the very best." "What's your source?" another blurted. The engineer named a ghetto near San Francisco. Between whoops of laughter, a good-looking Negro housewife said, "I collect Negroes, too. My source is my uterus." That was all it took. For a good ten minutes we had our laugh of relief. Gradually, we subsided into silence. Wearily we looked over toward Chuck. There still was work to be done. If Chuck had asked us to take the pressure off him, we would have. Or he could have simply left. The principle of the free learner applies strongly to encounter groups; leaving would constitute an honest and appropriate response. But we sensed that Chuck was as fascinated by the confrontation as we were. Just as he was gradually learning, so were we.

Another hour passed. At last, Chuck's voice was beginning to sound more natural. He was talking about his sexual prowess. "I could take any woman here," he said, his eyes flashing around the room.

"How would you take Pam?" I asked him.

"I'll tell you."

"Tell *her*."

He turned toward the teacher. "All right. First I'd rap you, then I'd take you."

"Rap?"

"Talk. You know, establish rapport. I'd rap you, then I'd take you."

Pam looked at him with scorn. "You'd never take me. I wouldn't let you *touch* me. *Ever.*"

"I'd take you, all right, baby." A fury lay just beneath his words.

Voices broke out around the group as various women denied or affirmed his sexual attraction. The Negro housewife leaned over toward him.

"You could never take me, and I'm going to tell you why." Something in her voice reduced us all to silence. "Because you're just a dirty little black nigger."

Chuck almost leaped from his chair. Clenching his fists on the armrests, he loosed his hidden fury in a savage and frightening tirade. Finally, he caught himself, looked around the room with dazed eyes and covered his face with his hands. He sat that way as members of the group comforted him. Then he looked up and smiled. His face was different.

A little later, after a surprisingly tender interchange, he said, "I want to thank all of you. I've learned more in the last two hours than in the last two years."

Near dawn, some of us went down through a dense fog to the baths. Others slept for an hour or two. All of us seemed illumined in the peculiar clarity of sleeplessness when we gathered in the meeting room after breakfast. Almost immediately, the group took an unexpected turn. The whites began revealing themselves, baring the most tragic and painful moments of their lives. *And the Negroes wept for the whites.* Without question of race, they *felt,* they *knew.* One after another, the revelations poured forth. The group took life of its own. There were no leaders now. We were all swept along.

An attractive white woman in her thirties had told us

brightly the first night that she had come to tape some inter-
views. Now she was telling us the real reason. She had a
half-Negro son. She hated the child's father, who had left
her, and she feared that she would become prejudiced
against the boy. The years were passing; she despaired of
ever getting another husband. The son hurt her chances
of remarriage. She resented Negro men and yet found
herself dating them.

"I'll tell you why I'm dating spades," she said, near
breakdown. "Because I've given up on white men." She
collapsed in racking sobs. Though her words might previously have been construed as prejudiced, it was a black
man who took her in his arms and comforted her.

Almost everyone in the room was crying. We were unashamed of our tears. We were not Negroes or whites or
Orientals. We were human beings joined in a very pre-
cious, fragile awareness of our common plight, of the waste
and loss in every life, and of hope for something better.
For many of us, that morning was transcendental, a space
in life when ordinary objects seem to shimmer, when all
faces are beautiful and time can be taken at the crest like
a great onrushing wave. That was the way it was for me.

Noon came and passed, but we wouldn't leave. At one-
thirty, the dining-room crew came and told us we would
have to go. We rose and moved, without a word, to the
center of the room in a mass, moist-eyed embrace.

Since then, Price and I had planned further racial confrontations in San Francisco, sponsored by Esalen and the
Episcopal Diocese of California. Other organizations have
taken up the idea, and like meetings are spreading through
the city. We can't predict what will eventually happen.
Perhaps some education will take place.

But the racial confrontation described was only one of

more than 650 Esalen meetings, each one unique and un-
predictable. Esalen remains truly experimental; if an
approach doesn't work, it is dropped, not made into a
rigid doctrine. It is a place where new things that don't
fit into the old structure can and do happen. One key reason may be that it is self-supporting, tied to no major corporation or foundation grant, and that it operates outside
the restrictive latticework of university academic depart-
ments. Though thirty-two of its forty-three officers and
advisors hold doctorates, the leadership is nonacademic—
whether the leader happens to have a "Dr." by his name
or not.

The Esalen experience shows that a new education is
possible. It is not important that educators, parents and
teachers follow the Esalen example or that they aim toward
a Kennedy School. It *is* important that they know they can
change more in their schools than the window dressing.
They have a real choice—now.

Earlier in this chapter, I mentioned that every new area
of education imagined for Kennedy School has been somehow explored at Esalen—with one exception. About that
exception: I cannot hang the blame for the fate of baseball
in the year 2001 on Esalen Institute or Michael Murphy.
Before starting Esalen, Murphy spent nine years of ascetic
study and contemplation in the Eastern disciplines. He
meditated six to eight hours a day for eighteen months
at the Sri Aurobindo *Ashram* in Pondicherry, India. He
came back to his native California convinced that the human potential, even in the realm called "mystical," can
best be achieved on an American model, through an affirmation of the sensory universe. His is an American
sadhana. Murphy, it must be revealed, is a good amateur
athlete and an avid sports fan. Dr. James Fadiman, a

brilliant young psychologist at Brandeis University, was once asked if he could sum up the "human potential movement" in a sentence. He considered the question for a moment, then answered: "I'd say it was Mike Murphy at a Giants game eating a hot dog and meditating."

The game with the flying disk is not an Esalen invention. It is one I have played for several years—mostly with novelists and journalists.

And now I must close this chapter. I hear from my transistor that the Giants and the Mets are tied in the top of the ninth. The game's on TV. McCovey's coming to bat.

grade classroom today resembles nothing so much as the classroom in which I daydreamed my way through second grade that year.

A certain caution in educational matters is quite understandable. A school child is far more complex, embodying far more variables, than NASA's entire satellite communications network. Baffled by this complexity and inhibited by a reluctance to "experiment" with children's lives, educators feel justified in clinging to methods that have been developed, hit or miss, over the centuries—even when those methods are shown to be inefficient. Others take refuge in education's old conservative function of passing along the culture's median knowledge, values and ways of perceiving —just when these things are shifting faster than we can perceive.

Where were the reformers who might have cried out in the wilderness of educational inertia? From the mid-fifties up until quite recently, most of them stood in the camps of reaction or conservatism. No need now to waste time on the Rickovers, Bestors and others of the Basic Education stripe. Their mindless assertions that education should be limited to "the mind" and their simplistic prescription that, to improve education, teachers merely need to know their subjects and "get tough" have done their damage— and have been repudiated. By exacerbating the conditions already existing in the schools, in fact, the reactionary critics have probably hastened the coming of real reform.

The conservative critics, on the other hand, may well bear some of the responsibility for delaying changes in education. Archetypical of these critics is the gray eminence, James B. Conant, a man of undoubted good credentials and good will. This establishment reformer, with enviable instruments of research and dissemination in his hands, regularly grinds out proposals for administrative and procedural repair, all the while treating the basic structure and content of U.S. education as if it were built to last a thousand years. His priorities reflect his background in higher education. He turns first to *high* school, is fascinated by subjects, tracks, units, administration. In writing that monument to the status quo *The American High School Today*, Dr. Conant simply overlooked the problems of the big-city slum school. He confessed this oversight in his belated *Slums and Suburbs*. By helping to shore up the present rickety educational structure with glue and plastic wood, such men as Conant inhibit educators from starting to build a new one.

More recently, an increasing number of less inhibiting voices have been raised. Student rebels and writers for underground newspapers have joined with critics such as Paul Goodman and Edgar Z. Friedenberg in impassioned outcries on what is stultifying and dehumanizing about our schools. They are incisive about what is wrong—especially at college level—but vague about what may be done to change things. Distrusting science, they often fail to credit recent experimental work in human learning that shows real reform is practical, not visionary.

But now it is clearly possible to opt for true alternatives, to build the new as well as to criticize the old. Every educator, parent and student has a stake in this building project. All will help determine whether our schools become flexible, humanistic and joyful, or whether they must first become more rigid, monolithic and doctrinaire. In either case, change they will. The old structure is crumbling. The traditional glue can't hold it together much longer. In building the new, we might start with three assumptions that by now may have a familiar ring:

1. *The human potential* is infinitely greater than we have been led to believe. *Acting* on this faith, we shall find that even small and simple efforts can yield us great gain

—efforts as small and simple as the experiment reported by psychologist Robert Rosenthal and school principal Lenore Jacobson in their book *Pygmalion in the Classroom*. The children in Dr. Jacobson's elementary school in South San Francisco were given IQ tests. Teachers were falsely told the tests would show which children would "spurt ahead" in their learning. The teachers (but not the parents or students) were given a list of twenty percent of the students. The children on the list were said to have great potential, but actually were selected randomly from all grades and all three achievement tracks. As it turned out, they *did* spurt ahead. For example, first-graders on the list gained an average 24.4 IQ points in one year, while members of the control group gained only 12 points. And these gains were accomplished even with the weak and crude educational techniques usually available. They resulted from nothing more than an assumption.

2. *Learning is sheer delight.* This doesn't mean it avoids tension or fears to look tragedy in the eye. But education devoid of the ecstatic moment is a mere shadow of education. We may assume that, when learners are apathetic, bored or just matter-of-fact, something is drastically wrong and that the wrong can be remedied.

3. *Learning itself is life's ultimate purpose.* This assumption has grave implications. If it is true, anyone who blocks learning, especially in a small child, is guilty of an enormous crime. The crimes against humanity, like the causes men are willing to fight and die for, do not appear all at once, absolute and sharply defined. Crimes and causes emerge gradually out of the clay of human experience. Noble Athenian ethics quite ignored the question of slavery. Tracts on American morality could omit consideration of segregation right up to the 1954 Supreme Court

decision and sometimes after. But once an outrage takes shape in our consciences, we are appalled—even as we reform it—at its enormity. Men have always been willing to put their lives on the line for things that have seemed essential to their lives—food, water, salt, land, freedom from slavery, better wages and working conditions, racial equality. And now, behold: Education emerges as the most essential. Today, schooling determines so much, even such matters as eventual earnings, status and neighborhood. But look beyond extrinsic rewards into the core of existence. In the future, a man's ability to learn and keep learning joyfully from birth to death will define the quality of life itself.

If this is the case, we should not be surprised and unprepared to wake up one morning to find riots and rebellion raging over the content, methods and goals of education. We have been warned: The student upheavals at large universities in recent years may have paraded under the banners of "free speech" and the like. But, make no mistake about it, they have been directed at the present institution of higher education itself. Though parents are only just now becoming aware of it, conditions in the early grades are far more crucial. The experiments of Krech at Berkeley, showing that educational deprivation actually stunts the growth of the cerebral cortex (see Chapter II), are being validated at more and more laboratories. *Your child robbed of his brain tissue?* Here is something— though the notion may seem a quaint one to the old revolutionaries of the thirties—about which people may someday shed blood.

But bloodshed, violence, revolution are not the way to educational reform in this age. An outrage overthrown by an outrage generally gives birth to an outrage. Conventional mass movements, with militant demonstrations, banners and simplistic slogans, often lend new life to the extreme positions they oppose. The conditions of living in the U.S. have become too complex and interrelated for the either/or, *us* vs. *them*, highly polarized modes of change. The new technology brings us new modes of change. Increasing interdependence along with fast, continent-wide communication media make possible the rapid spread of appealing and workable new alternatives.

We start, then, not merely by attacking existing educational environments, but by building new ones. How? The ways are many.

A foundation or other funding agency interested in changing the face of American education now has that opportunity. It will do so not by sponsoring a technological spectacular (say, orbiting airplanes to relay classroom TV across several states) or by paying for expensive and ponderous national assessments that measure the effectiveness of things-as-they-are. Instead, the innovative agency (or group of agencies) can help set up a half dozen early-education schools, starting with the four years from three through six and adding a new age group every year. These schools might start with principles such as those explored in the preceding chapters. But they would by no means seek standardization. Each would be encouraged to grow organically, to learn from its learners. They might vary widely as to geographical region and type of neighborhood. Up to three of the six might be located in ghettos, and I would expect the "deprived" children here to outperform students in the best conventional suburban schools, on their own terms, as well as doing things conventional educators have not dreamed of. Most important, all of this would be accomplished *without any of the usual pressures on the learners whatever.*

"Faculties" in the model schools would not be limited

to professional educators. The professionals would be welcomed. But they, like all others involved, would have to show their willingness and ability to break set, to help create a new, ever-changing climate of learning. People from diverse fields would be invited to participate, especially members of the burgeoning new breed of generalists —that is, competent and knowledgeable people whose perceptions and actions are not limited by specialized boundaries.

On the specialist-generalist question, communicator Howard Gossage, a self-proclaimed generalist, has written:

> Once you take a problem to a specialist, you're wired into a specialist's solution. Let us say your company is having growing pains and is uncomfortable in its present quarters. So you go to an architect. He inquires after your needs, your ambitions, your hopes, your fears, what manner of people you are, etc. Do you know what you're going to end up with? A building.
>
> Now, a building, however nice, may not be the answer to your problem at all. Perhaps the real answer is to stop expanding, or to fire the president, or that everyone should stay home and do cottage work connected by closed-circuit TV. But these are generalist solutions, not the sort of thing you'd expect an architect to come up with.

It might be added that today every specialty harbors secret generalists. The new education will help flush them out into the open.

Up against the giant bulk of the U.S. education establishment, a half dozen experimental schools may not sound like much. But in the electronic networks and the national magazines we have something new in human history: a way to speak with a single voice to a continent-wide society. Startling news travels wide and fast. The media can create a climate for change. With educators, parents and students looking for new approaches, six radically different —and successful—schools could transform education everywhere.

But this is only one of a spectrum of strategies. Changes can come one step at the time. Teachers can work toward making their own classrooms into free-learning environments and can create there new modes of human relations. They can start with something as simple as taping a classroom discussion. The playback is a revelation to most teachers. They are amazed to learn how much they talk, how little chance their students have to respond. Teachers can also gain useful feedback in encounter-group sessions. Several encounter experiments are underway in U.S. public and parochial schools in an attempt to get teachers ready for change. One of the experimenters, Dr. Carl Rogers of the Western Behavioral Sciences Institute, is working with the school system run by the Immaculate Heart Sisters. He plans eventually to involve everyone in some sixty elementary and secondary schools—and this includes administrators, teacher trainers, faculty, students, parents, community leaders and dropouts. Dr. George I. Brown of the University of California at Santa Barbara is using sensory awareness, bodily movements and other techniques as well as encounter in an Esalen program for public-school teachers funded by the Ford Foundation.

Many teachers who have attended Esalen Institute workshops or other innovative practice sessions have returned to their schools to transform their own classes, to influence their colleagues' by example. This has not necessarily been in the nature of subversion. Administrators sometimes have responded sympathetically to experimentation and have followed up the pioneering teachers' quest for a new education.

True, educational administrators often hesitate to rock the boat. They feel themselves hemmed in by all sorts of constraints—school boards, teachers' associations, lobby groups that pressure for selfish and often contradictory causes. They tend, therefore, to consider the course of least action the safest. But when they sense a lessening of these constraints, administrators, "educationists," can become enthusiastic sponsors of reforms that increase the freedom and learning ability of their students.

In fact, the educationists' most rabid detractors may turn out to be the real Philistines of an age that demands change. These may even include a few cultured, literate men and women who cling so desperately to "good taste" that they cannot bear the inevitable gropings that accompany every pioneering effort; who sense a little spurt of smug warmth when Faulkner concludes that the "Ode on a Grecian Urn" is worth any number of old ladies; who fear nothing so much as enthusiasm and value nothing so much as irony—defined by author Wallace Stegner as "that curse, that evasion, that armor, that way of staying safe while seeming wise." Underrate the educators at your own risk. The post-World War II crop is the best in memory. When the public is ready, they will move. In my judgment, that time has come.

Students and faculty in the upper grades and in college can also move into new educational modes, if they are willing to build anew, not just criticize the old. San Francisco State's Experimental College is a good example. In a period of two years, this student-led experiment has not only carried on a large and spirited program of its own, but has strongly influenced its parent college as well. An Experimental College bulletin described the concept behind the enterprise:

The idea is that students ought to take responsibility for their own education. The assertion is that you can start learning anywhere, as long as you really care about the problem that you tackle and how well you tackle it. The method is one which asks you to learn how you learn. . . . The assumption is that you are capable of playing a major role in evaluating your own performance. The claim is that if people, students, faculty, and administrators, work with each other in these ways, that the finest quality education will occur. The Experimental College was built to develop a new style of learning and teaching, to serve as a model for the direction in which San Francisco State College might grow.

Anyone who wished—student, faculty member, outsider —could attempt to start a course on anything he wished; the course would become a reality if enough students came to it. Up to 1,200 students have been enrolled. Within the limitations of the classes-courses model, the Experimental College has moved a long way toward encounter, exploration and free learning. And its innovations have been snapped up eagerly by perhaps a majority of the faculty and administration of San Francisco State.

This success contrasts with the Free Speech Movement at nearby Berkeley, which primarily succeeded in helping elect a hostile state administration. James Nixon, onetime president of State's Associated Students, worked first along the lines of the Free Speech Movement. Learning from his FSM experience, he then became instrumental in setting up the Experimental College. He tells how the two operations differed:

The FSM showed it was possible to act and have impact. It created the vacuum that we tried to fill. But when I identified with the FSM, I perceived the establishment as completely hostile. I felt it was behind a high wall and there was no way I could communicate with it. So I had to demonstrate, picket, sit in. I defined and therefore limited myself by my opposition to the establishment. So—it turned out the establishment *was* hostile. It *was* monolithic. It *was* behind a high wall and I *couldn't* communicate with it.

Then, when we got the idea of the Experimental College, I started by perceiving the establishment as possibly friendly, as something I *could* communicate with. And we went on to build a structure of our own right inside the establishment so that we would have something to offer, something of value to communicate. From the beginning, we assumed a dialogue with the establishment would be possible. So it turned out that at least a part of the establishment *was* friendly, we *could* communicate with it and the dialogue *did* happen.

Today, indeed, San Francisco State is fast changing from a little-known streetcar college to a nationally known center of innovation in higher education.

Again and again it turns out that reforms *are* possible, inside and outside of established institutions, when the reformers assume the best and then act, when they build rather than just protest. It is not necessary to wait for official approval at every level. It is not necessary to wait for experts. In fact, one of the most significant findings of the Western Behavioral Sciences Institute has been that encounter groups operating without professionals have been able to achieve (among other things) therapeutic results that certainly equal those of professional therapy. The Institute's director, Dr. Richard Farson, points out, "In spite of compelling evidence, we generally fail to attend to the greatest resource we have for the solution of every social problem—that is, the very population that has the problem." Farson cites Synanon and Alcoholics Anonymous as examples that former dope addicts and alcoholics are best at fighting those problems. "And research evidence from a variety of sources indicates that convicts themselves leading rehabilitation programs have shown a better rehabilitative record in working with convicts than have the correction officers and other specialists who have previously guided the programs. In the ghettos, too, the best results have come from Community Action Programs that have put the control of Negroes' destiny in their own hands. Perhaps this is the true meaning of Black Power—a drive for self-respect through self-help." Dr. Farson estimates that over 1,000 self-help organizations now are functioning in the U.S., from A.A. to Parents Without Partners.

Their success in dealing with human difficulties suggests that self-help can also succeed in moving people toward higher orders of life. Farson has proposed that married couples form networks to monitor each others' marriages and provide honest feedback on how they can be improved. As it is now, his research has shown, the Browns can plainly see what needs to be done to improve the Jones' marriage. And the Jones can evaluate the Browns' just as readily and accurately. But neither couple, under the present mode of relating, dares to tell the other. Farson's new network would encourage openness and encounter, and could serve as the foundation for a vast interpersonal experiment to increase the enjoyment of life and elicit an ever-increasing amount of human potential.

Indeed, the modern family, encouraged by other families and pursuing uncommon goals of human accomplishment, can become perhaps the most powerful agency of education and the reform of education. Parents have the very first opportunity to create joyful and effective learning environments for their children. From the beginning they can reinforce exploratory behavior in every child.

Sometimes this may seem a little hard on furniture, but, to turn Faulkner around, a happy, free-learning child is worth any number of broken ashtrays. Anyway, discipline and the acknowledgment of necessary limits are not incompatible with free learning. Certain areas of a house can be designated free-learning areas, where almost everything goes. Parents who are truly in touch with their children can set up the kinds of environments that will bring forth remarkably constructive and involving behaviors. In our house we have used a central room (once the dining room) for this purpose. It contains worktables, musical instruments, tape recorders, art and craft materials, children's books and the sort of miscellany and junk that children use to create their own worlds. The key to making such an environment work, we have found, is to resist becoming "teachers." The parents' task is to keep expanding the environment, the possibilities; to introduce materials that, as in the Kennedy Discovery Tents, stretch but don't lose the child. This takes ingenuity. If the situation is programmed skillfully, you will almost always run out of environment before running out of your child's ability to cope with it.

With automation, increasing amounts of human energy are rapidly becoming available. Individuals, families and organizations now have the opportunity to create new cultures within a lifetime, to burnish anew the hopes, the goals that brought this nation into being. There is little time for delay. We may have reached the moment in history, as many have suggested, where the basic alternatives lie somewhere between sweeping reform and self-destruction. The future guarantees no kindness to those who, in the name of "reasonableness" or "practicality" or out of fear of being thought presumptuous, fail to make the larger proposals.

I am reminded here of the only meeting I had with Aldous Huxley. It was a blazing California day in June of 1962, seventeen months before his death on November 22, 1963. We sat in lawn chairs in the Hollywood Hills. A yellowish haze dazzled the sky. Hundreds of thousands of cars were rushing along freeways, roads, streets that stretched for miles around us. Thick tropical foliage screened the cars from our view. We were aware only of their sound, a distant rush of wind. Huxley was a slim, elegant man of nearly seventy, but his mind was youthful and eager as he leaned forward, head cocked to the side, struggling with the questions we had put to each other.

"When I wrote *Brave New World* in 1932," Huxley said, "I had no idea how soon so much of it would come true. I had no *idea*—I don't think anyone did—how swiftly science would develop, how fast the population would increase, how effectively people would be organized in larger and larger groups. Already, we're working out most of the techniques for controlling the mind, as I saw them in my book. What's more, our power for controlling—or devastating—the outside world already has proceeded beyond what I could have foreseen."

Huxley, a prophet surpassed by reality, gestured around him. "Look at Los Angeles. You can see it all here—the poisoning of the water and the air itself, the rape of the open country, the depletion of farmland for housing. Mankind should not fear a Martian invasion. We are our own Martians. With the help of science and technology, we are destroying much of what is beautiful and valuable on this planet. You must tell people they don't have much time. We all must start thinking like mad. We must *do* something."

"But *what* shall we do?" I asked him. "*What* shall I tell people?"

"That's hard to say. The Founding Fathers of this country were concerned with the sources of power of that time and with humane restraint of that power. Now new sources of power have developed—enormously greater than anything previously imagined. I feel we need some kind of new Constitutional Convention, a new meeting of 'Founding Fathers' who will take steps to insure that the power released by science will not limit human freedom or destroy the world."

"Yes, but how are we to organize such a convention?" I asked.

"It would be difficult, of course."

"In the meantime, what specific steps do you think we should take? What shall we do to stave off what clearly seems to be certain disaster?"

"I just don't know," the prophet said.

Since that meeting (which set me thinking about writing this book), I have gone back to our conversation many times. Much has happened during the intervening years. Since Huxley's death, the alternatives have become clearer. Perhaps if he were alive today, he might help us set up, in fact, a new "Constitutional Convention." It could start with meetings at local, then state levels. It could involve not only governmental officials, but interested citizens from all walks of life. It could take a *completely fresh look* at the "humane uses of power," beyond all the traditional solutions. It could assume that workable new solutions do exist, that we do have the resources and can develop the techniques to make these solutions work. The statewide meetings could lead to a series of national meetings in Washington, not to write a new constitution, but perhaps to draw up documents and guidelines for action concerning rights to *quality* in life—the rights to clean air and water, to natural beauty, to privacy and uniqueness in an electronic world and—most especially—the right to education in the broad, new sense of the word. Even now, in an age of universal education, schools can accomplish what Utopia never could.

Already, fragments of this work are being accomplished at various conferences cn the future. But a truly national effort to define new alternatives, sponsored by both the private and public sectors, could electrify the nation and the world, and set us off on a new footing. Our worst error would lie in dreaming too small.

the old sense have been annihilated. The whole globe is intimately intertwined with the means for achieving understanding or destruction.

This situation, despite attempts at drawing historical parallels, cannot be viewed simply as more of the same. It is something entirely new, calling for entirely new responses. What is more important, it seems to demand a new kind of human being—one who is not driven by narrow competition, eager acquisition and aggression, but who spends his life in the joyful pursuit of learning. Such a human being, I feel, will result not so much through changed ideologies or economic systems as through changes in the process I have called "education." The idea of education as the most effective human change agent is by no means new. But I have tried to broaden and simplify education's definition, to expand its domain, to link it with the new technology and to alter the relationship between educator and learner. As a chief ingredient in all this, as well as an alternative to the old reinforcers, I have named "ecstasy"—joy, *ananda*, the ultimate delight.

Our society knows little about this ingredient. In fact, every civilization in our direct lineage has tended to fear and shun it as a threat to reason and order. In a sense, they have been right. It is hard to imagine a more revolutionary statement for us than "The natural condition of the human organism is joy." For, if this is true, we are being daily cheated, and perhaps the social system that so ruthlessly steals our birthright *should* be overthrown.

How many of us can live through three or four utterly joyful days without feeling, shortly afterwards, that our plane will crash or that we shall be struck with lightning? It is deeply embedded, this societal teaching. And when a highly visible segment of our young people, sometimes through shortsighted means, devotes all its days and nights to the pursuit of joy, how many of us do not feel deeply threatened? Joy *does* threaten things-as-they-are. Ecstasy, like nuclear energy, *is* dangerous. The only thing that may turn out to be more dangerous is shunning it and clinging to the old ways that clearly are dragging us toward destruction.

Perhaps it is time for scholars and pundits to engage in the serious study of delight. What are its dangers? What are its uses? I would suggest three primarily negative considerations as a beginning:

1. *Ecstasy is not necessarily opposed to reason.* On the other hand, it may help light the way toward relationships, societies and educational systems in which reason and emotion are no longer at odds; in which, in fact, the two are so in tune that the terms themselves, as opposites, will atrophy.

2. *Ecstasy is not necessarily opposed to order.* On the other hand, it may help us redefine order. In the new definition, a balanced natural ecology in which all creatures grow and act freely represents order. Our free-learning and joyful Kennedy School represents a far higher, more elegant form of order than does a school in which "order" is forced and artificial. Life is an ordering force. Man is an ordering animal. Order will continue to evolve. Ecstasy is implicated in changing not the quantity, but the quality of order.

3. *Ecstasy is neither immoral nor moral in itself.* At times, forms of ecstasy have powered some of mankind's most destructive movements. The Third Reich, for example, exhibited a certain ecstatic mania. But Hitler's "joy" was used to bolster the old reinforcement system—

competition, acquisition and aggression—carried to the most destructive extremes. It was not brought into play as an *alternative* reinforcement system designed to replace the old.

In dealing with ecstasy, as with all powerful forces, context is crucial. The context I have suggested is neither the wantonly Dionysian nor the purely contemplative, but the educational. Ecstasy is education's most powerful ally. It is reinforcer for and substance of the moment of learning.

Knowing this, the master teacher pursues delight. Even those best known as great lecturers have turned their lecture halls into theaters, shameless in their use of spells and enchantments. Great men, as every schoolboy knows, have greeted their moments of learning with crazy joy. We learn how Archimedes leaped, crying, "Eureka!," from his bathtub; how Handel, on finishing the "Hallelujah Chorus," told his servant, "I did think I did see all Heaven before me, and the great God himself"; how Nietzsche wrote *Thus Spake Zarathustra*:

> There is an ecstasy such that the immense strain of it is sometimes relaxed by a flood of tears, along with which one's steps either rush or involuntarily lag, alternately. There is the feeling that one is completely out of hand, with the very distinct consciousness of an endless number of fine thrills and quiverings to the very toes.

What we fail to acknowledge is that every child starts out as an Archimedes, a Handel, a Nietzsche. The eight-month-old who succeeds in balancing one block on another has made a connection no less momentous for him than Nietzsche's. He cannot verbalize it so eloquently and probably would not bother to if he could; such moments are not so rare for him as for Nietzsche. Much of his life at that age, in fact, is learning. The possibility of an endless series of ecstatic moments stretches before him. We quell the ecstasy and the learning, but this is hard work and rarely is it entirely successful. Explaining why he was unable to think about scientific problems for a year after his final exams, Albert Einstein said:

> It is in fact nothing short of a miracle that the modern methods of instruction have not yet entirely strangled the holy curiosity of inquiry. . . . It is a very grave mistake to think that the enjoyment of seeing and searching can be promoted by means of coercion and a sense of duty.

And yet, life and joy cannot be subdued. The blade of grass shatters the concrete. The spring flowers bloom in Hiroshima. An Einstein emerges from the European academies. Those who would reduce, control, quell must lose in the end. The ecstatic forces of life, growth and change are too numerous, too various, too tumultuous.

In the eighteenth century, the Swedish botanist Carolus Linnaeus thought he had catalogued all the species of animals and plants in the world, a total of 4,345. He was wrong. Biologists today estimate they have classified nearly two million different kinds of animals; botanists have identified more than 300,000 kinds of plants. And that is only a beginning. Entomologists believe that, if all forms of insects alone could be counted, they would total from two to ten million. Faced with this profusion, scientists have run out of suitable Latin and Greek names, and now grope for impressive-sounding words that mean nothing whatever in any language. And all this life, the affirmation of development and change, has taken place in the surface film of an average-size planet of an average-size star in one of hundreds of millions of galaxies. If this planet were the size of an orange, the habitat of all living things would be no thicker than a piece of paper.

Life has one ultimate message, "Yes!" repeated in infinite number and variety. Human life, channeled for millennia by Civilization, is only just beginning to express the diversity and range of which it is easily capable. To deny is to swim against the current of existence. To affirm, to follow ecstasy in learning—in spite of injustice, suffering, confusion and disappointment—is to move more easily toward an education, a society that would free the enormous potential of man.

July the Fourth. A lake in the Georgia woods. The soft, still air of afternoon vibrates with a thousand lives: the mad, monotonous trance music of the cicadas rising and falling above the chatter of crickets, the drone of bees; cries of a Cooper's hawk on a dead tree across the lake; birdsong all around, a different blend for every change of sky or air. The acoustics are incredible. Sound floats across the lake, touches me, immediate and eternal. All is one and I am of that one.

I walk slowly toward the lake's edge. A blacksnake whistles away through high grasses. A pair of white herons that have been working their way around the borders of the lake rise with undulating, confident strokes. Disdainful, taking their own time, they fly on to a spot appropriately distant from me. *Perfect.* Over the water, a flycatcher shoots straight upward with wings fluttering fast, then spreading motionless at the apogee—a moment frozen in thin air. A buzzard, an inverted shadow, cruises overhead. And there on a slim pine branch (pine needles spread like star points) a tiny warbler is silhouetted, upside down.

A turtle rests on the bank. I pick it up. Dark brown shell; long, translucent bear claws clawing air. A yellow spotted head lengthens, cranes around. Impersonal eyes see nothing, see everything. I return the turtle to its bank.

Squatting down, I watch a dragonfly less than an inch long with wings like amber cellophane quivering on a weed in the burnt gold of late afternoon.

What now? A green grasshopper, disturbed by my movements, has jumped into the lake. He kicks as in a spasm, then lies in the water. Two ripples move out, concentric circles signaling his plight. He kicks again, moving toward the tangled bank. Will he make it? Two more spasmodic kicks and he's in shallow water. The bottom is visible. Almost safe. And the fish is there, a light shadow appearing, fully in position, without movement. Though only as long as a hand, the fish is somehow terribly sinister. *Snakkk!* A sharp report, a mouth sound. Empty water.

Later, just before the sun goes down, blue shadows settle into the spaces beneath the trees across the lake. The sky is a confusion of shifting clouds and colors. With twilight's advance, the colors richen, the sky comes to rest. After sundown, I take a rowboat out onto the water. The air is cooling, the trees are utterly still. White morning glories on the bank are closed for the night. Turtles peep out of the still water, curious rather than predatory. A wood thrush sings, its trill swelling suddenly to fill all the evening like a distended balloon. A wren sings, a cardinal, a warbler— all sweet singers.

Darkness approaches. The songs end. Something is swimming, making steady progress along the shore toward my boat. The swimmer goes into the bank for a moment, curves out again, its ripples making a precise triangle behind it. It sees me, dives. And now I know the night hunters have awakened. Two frogs croak tentatively. A night hawk sweeps across the lake. I can barely make out a possum moving deliberately along the opposite bank. I head the boat back toward the bank. The lake is a faint gleam, the trees black silhouettes.

This world is elegantly interconnected and all-involving. It cannot be compartmentalized. It does not cease.

William Golding's novel of some years back, *Lord of the Flies,* generally has been interpreted as a bitter commentary on man's nature. In it, a group of children, marooned on a deserted island, turn from Ralph, the voice of Civilized reason, and Piggy, his myopic egghead sidekick, to join Jack, who has been interpreted as the villain, the savage, the dark spirit in man that invariably emerges when the Civilized restraints are removed.

But Golding stacked the deck in a way that comments more on Civilization than on "human nature." Ralph is "good," but dull, unimaginative and indecisive. Piggy has "mind," but not much else. He is physically and sensorially inept. Jack, on the other hand, is physically and mentally alert, resourceful, imaginative and creative. He encourages his followers in games and chants, colorful costumes and face paint, ceremonies and a sense of community. He organizes successful pig hunts and provides his meat-hungry children with torchlit feasts. Meanwhile, Ralph and his dispirited followers sicken on their unvarying diet of fruit. What child would not follow Jack? When Golding makes Jack's group evil, he reveals the usual inability in our time to equate the ecstatic with the good. When he makes Civilized Ralph dull and inept, he reveals what he really feels about Civilization as he knows it.

When men must serve as predictable, prefabricated components of a rigid social machine, the ecstatic is not particularly useful and may, in fact, erode the compartments so necessary for the machine's functioning. But when a society moves away from the mechanistic, when an individual may function as a free-roving seeker, when what we now term "leisure" occupies most of an individual's hours, ecstasy may usefully accompany almost every act. Technology is preparing a world in which we may be learners all life long. In this world, delight will not be a luxury but a necessity.

I can recall little of what happened in school the winter I was fifteen. Perhaps that was the year everyone in my English class had to do a chapter-by-chapter synopsis of *Treasure Island*. But the afternoons and nights of that period still are vivid. I was infected with the ham-radio bug. My next-door neighbor, a boy two years older, had got me started, and I lived for months in a state of delicious excitement. I would rush home from school, knowing the day would not be long enough. I would work steadily, practicing code, devouring ham manuals and magazines, poring over catalogues of radio parts, building simple shortwave receivers. I loved everything about it. When later I read Gerard Manley Hopkins' "Pied Beauty," the phrase, "all trades, their gear and tackle and trim," immediately summoned up the coils and condensers, the softly glowing vacuum tubes, the sizzle and smell of hot solder, the shining curls of metal drilled out of a chassis.

One night, my radio experience came to a moment of climax. For weeks I had been working on my first major effort, a four-tube regenerative shortwave receiver. The design was "my own," derived from circuits in the manuals and approved by my knowledgeable friend. Every part was of the highest quality, all housed in a professional-looking black metal cabinet. Every knob and dial was carefully positioned for efficiency and esthetics, and there was an oversized, freewheeling band-spread tuning knob. That particular night I had been working ever since running most of the way home from school. I had skipped dinner, fiercely overriding my parents' protests. And now, at about eleven o'clock, I soldered the last connection.

With trembling hands, I connected the ground and the antenna, plugged in the socket and switched on the set. There was a low, reassuring hum and, after a suspenseful wait, the four tubes lit up. I increased the volume. Dead silence. Nothing. I checked all the switches and dials. No problem there. Perhaps it was the speaker. I plugged in the earphones. Still nothing.

I couldn't imagine what was the matter. For the next hour or so, I went over every connection, traced the circuit until I was dizzy. Since I had splurged on all-new parts, I didn't even consider that one of them might be defective. The mystery, so powerful and unfathomable, could obviously have been cleared up in a few minutes by any well-equipped radio repairman. But, for me, its unraveling was momentous.

The radio's circuit consisted of two stages. The first stage converted radio frequency waves to electrical impulses of an audible frequency; the second stage served as an amplifier for the electrical impulses coming from the first stage. I hit upon the idea of tapping the earphones in at the end of the first stage. Success! Static, code, voices. This seemed to indicate to me that the trouble lay somewhere in the second stage. On an impulse, however, I tied in a microphone at the very beginning of the second stage. Success again. The second stage worked. I could hear my voice coming from the speaker.

At that very instant, the answer was clear: Both stages worked separately. The trouble had to lie in the coupling between them. My eyes went to a little green and silver coil (*the broken connection between subconscious and conscious, the hidden flaw between individual and community*). It *had* to be that impedance coil. With this certainty, I was quite overcome. I would gladly have broken into a radio store to get another one, but my friend, I found, had a spare. I tied it in, not bothering for the moment to solder it. And a universe poured into my room from the star-filled night. I spun the dial: a ham in Louisiana, in California; shortwave broadcasts from England, Germany, Mexico, Brazil. There was no end to it. I had put out new sensors. Where there had been nothing, there was *all of this*.

Ecstasy is one of the trickier conditions to write about. But if there is such a thing as being transported, I was transported that night. And I was, as with every true learning experience, forever afterwards changed.

Every child, every person can delight in learning. A new education is already here, thrusting up in spite of every barrier we have been able to build. Why not help it happen?